# Before the Premier League
A History of the Football League's Last Decades

**PAUL WHITTLE**

# Before the Premier League
A History of the Football League's Last Decades

**PAUL WHITTLE**

# Before the Premier League
A History of the Football League's Last Decades
**© Paul Whittle**

Paul Whittle has asserted his rights in accordance with the Copyright, Designs & Patents Act 1988 to be identified to be the author of this work.

Published by:
**Wibble Publishing**

British Columbia, Canada

Email: info@wibblepublishing.com
Web: www.wibblepublishing.com

First published 2021

All rights reserved. All images, texts, and contents within this book are subject to copyright laws. No part of this publication may be reproduced, stored in a retrieval system now known or hereafter invented, or transmitted in any form or by any means, electronic, mechanical, photocopying, recording or otherwise, without the prior permission in writing of the publisher and the copyright owners.

Legal Deposit: Library and Archives Canada, Ottawa, Ontario, Canada.

13-digit ISBN: 978-1-987860-44-3

Printed in Great Britain

# Acknowledgements

The initial inspiration for this book came from reading R. C. Churchill's *Sixty Seasons of League Football*. I first discussed it with my then-colleague Richard High, with the idea of a statistically-based study, before it gradually took shape as a more rounded history. Since then, I have had very helpful feedback on early drafts from Peter Lythe, and Oliver and Janet Pickering, and useful discussions with Gavin Buckland. Gavin and all interviewees generously gave their time to speak with me at length, and their input has been invaluable.

Thanks to Pete Hurn and John Dewhirst for advice, and John's kind permission to use his original photographs, alongside Peter Court (courtesy of James Court) and Steve McGhee. Duncan Holley, Andy Dakin and David Williams also kindly made images from their personal collections available to me. Many thanks go to Dave and Rick at Wibble Publishing for all their efforts in editing, formatting and making the book a reality.

I have corresponded with many people about different aspects of the book, whether to answer specific queries, for help in contacting players or sourcing images. There are too many to thank individually, but all assistance has been greatly appreciated.

Special thanks go to Joe Sargison, a childhood friend and now FA Coach Educator, for his encouragement and enthusiasm throughout. Joe also provided introductions for my first interviews, which otherwise would not have been possible for me to arrange. Finally, many thanks to Harry, Max and my wife Jane for her unwavering support in what proved to be a long-term project, indulging football discussions, library visits, reading and regular viewing of old videos in the name of research.

**Image Credits**:

[Cover, top] 1. Roker Park, Sunderland (Sunderland v Bradford City, Division Two 1984/85). Copyright John Dewhirst.

[Cover, bottom] 2. Molineux, Wolverhampton (Wolves v Charlton Athletic, Division Two 1991/92). Copyright Peter Court, courtesy of James Court.

3. The Dell, Southampton (Southampton v Sunderland, FA Cup 1961/62). Courtesy of The Duncan Holley Collection.

4. The Dell, Southampton (Southampton v Charlton Athletic, Division Two 1965/66). Courtesy of The Duncan Holley Collection.

5. Burnden Park, Bolton (Bolton Wanderers v Blackburn Rovers, Division One 1960/61). Courtesy of David Williams.

6. Belle Vue, Doncaster (c. mid-1980s). Copyright Steve McGhee.

7. Sealand Road, Chester (c. early 1990s). Copyright Andy Dakin.

8. Goldstone Ground, Brighton (Brighton v Bradford City, Division Two 1984/85). Copyright John Dewhirst.

9. Filbert Street, Leicester (Leicester City v Charlton Athletic, Division One 1986/87). Copyright Peter Court, courtesy of James Court.


Every effort has been made to credit copyright holders, but in several instances none have been identified despite a diligent search having been carried out. If you have information about the identity or the location of the copyright holder(s), please contact the author via www.the1888letter.com

# Before the Premier League
A History of the Football League's Last Decades

| | |
|---|---|
| Introduction | 9 |
| | |
| Structure of the Football League | 13 |
| An Overview of the First Sixty Seasons of League Football | 16 |
| Timeline | 20 |

## The Final Period of the Football League: 1958-1992

| | |
|---|---|
| From Churchill to the 1960s | 23 |
| The Transfer Market (Part One) | 32 |
| The 1970s | 37 |
| Sponsorship | 49 |
| The Transfer Market (Part Two) | 54 |
| The 1980s | 57 |
| Attendances | 69 |
| Television | 74 |
| Conclusion | 79 |

## Statistics

| | |
|---|---|
| Top Scorers by Season | 87 |
| Major English Records | 93 |
| Individual Player & Club Records | 101 |
| | |
| Interviews | 106 |
| | |
| Bibliography | 214 |

# Introduction

"English League football is a typical product of English life, and in nothing is it more typical than in the fact that it was founded by a Scotsman and that many of its best players have always come from Ireland, Scotland and Wales." R.C. Churchill, *Sixty Seasons of League Football*

This book covers the major changes and events during the last thirty-four years of the Football League, before the breakaway of the Premier League in 1992. It was roughly intended as a sequel to R.C. Churchill's *Sixty Seasons of League Football*, published in 1958 by Penguin Books, which covered the history of the Football League from its formation in 1888 to the start of the 1958/59 season.

At the time of writing, there are less Englishmen – Scots, Welsh and Irish likewise – playing in the top division of English football than ever before. Churchill, author of the study *A Short History of the Future* in addition to the seminal *Sixty Seasons of League Football,* could surely not have anticipated such a state of affairs. He was able to look back on those first sixty seasons, spanning the Victorian era to the eve of the 1960s, and note a remarkable degree of continuity.

The Football League, founded by a Scot, William McGregor, introduced the notion of professional football as a commercial business. While the early years had their share of scandal – undeclared payments, 'poaching' of players, rule-bending, bribery, corruption and greed – the concept of the League itself was universally accepted. The League was a commercial enterprise, but the integrity of the competition was actively protected, and those who sought an unfair advantage ran the risk of often draconian punishments. Clubs such as Aston Villa and Manchester City were sanctioned for breaching regulations and one of the game's biggest names, Billy Meredith,[1] was banned for a full season.

Yet the Football League largely preserved its social function and original, collective ethos, which for 104 years from its inception enshrined wealth re-distribution throughout the divisions, protected and regulated for the benefit of all its member clubs as representatives of their local communities. Less than half a century later, the continuity of English league football, which both Churchill and Arthur Hopcraft,[2] a respected journalist writing in the sixties, remarked upon, has been broken.

The roots of the game, its development in the nineteenth century, the creation and expansion of the League, its early years and growth in popularity up to the 1950s, is exhaustively documented by Churchill and later writers on the game such as Simon Inglis,[3] Mark Metcalf[4] and others. It is a fascinating story in its own right and I have only given a brief overview of those first sixty seasons, separated by the two World Wars.

Churchill's book concludes when the League moved to four national divisions for the first time in 1958, replacing the former Third Divisions North and South. This book brings that history to a close at the end of the 1991/92 season, the last to feature a unified League of 92 clubs comprising Divisions One to Four, before the formation of the Premier League. English league football was to undergo the final stage of its transformation, from a primarily working-class sport developed in the industrial heartlands, to global corporate entertainment.

Observers from the 1950s right up to the 80s could recognise the game's Victorian origins in its stadia, stands and terraces, its communal spirit and egalitarian principles of revenue-sharing, in contests between teams numbered 1-11 on heavy pitches with even heavier tackling. An era when a club's owners were little-known, seldom seen or heard of; income was largely generated through the turnstiles; seven-figure transfer fees a sensation;

---

1 A Welsh international who won major trophies with both Manchester clubs and instigator of the first Players' Union.
2 Author of *The Football Man: People and Passions in Soccer* (1968)
3 Simon Inglis, *League Football and the Men who Made it: The Official Centenary History of the Football League, 1888-1988* (Harper Collins, 1988)
4 Mark Metcalf, *The Origins of the Football League: The First Season 1888/89* (Amberley, 2013)

televised football and players from overseas a rarity; the FA Cup Final the centre-piece of the domestic football calendar and the First Division title the English game's most prestigious and keenly-contested honour. That world has vanished, replaced by a corporate entity with global reach operating under the trade name of the English Premier League (EPL), which would be unrecognisable to football followers of earlier generations.

Howard Wilkinson's Leeds United won the First Division in 1991/92, the final season of an intact Football League; with the Premier League entering its fourth decade, he remains the last English manager to achieve the feat. The subsequent years have seen English football's top division enjoy unprecedented commercial success and tap into a global market, broadcast to vast worldwide television audiences. However, I believe the decision to create a new division marked the end of an era, not only in name but as a fundamentally different competition; one which represents a decisive break in continuity and unity from the notion of a Football League as envisaged at its founding by McGregor, and maintained for over a century. At the top level, clubs owned by the mega-rich amass vast squads, hoarding players from across the globe, while enjoying ever-growing profits. Below this, in the re-named Championship, Leagues One and Two (formerly Divisions Two to Four), the remaining seventy-two teams compete for scraps from the Premier League; fears of bankruptcy, poverty and winding-up orders are the norm for the bulk of these clubs.

The Premier League was the culmination of trends of commercialisation and globalisation, the growing influence of television and big business over decades, but taken to a new and hitherto unimaginable level. It has been, in purely financial terms, hugely successful; thanks in large part to the colossal sums paid by television companies for viewing rights and associated commercial deals, its players are paid and transferred for astronomical amounts, whilst managers also earn greater salaries than ever before. The Premier League era is symbolised by widespread moves to new, purpose-built stadia named for their major sponsors, removing clubs from their histories and, in many cases, the communities which once sustained them. In addition to the players, the majority of current top-level managers are from overseas, as are the owners of the clubs.

Generations have grown up knowing only the current model of league football; this book attempts to redress the balance. In his book, Churchill designated three periods of the League, divided by the Wars – the first 1888-1915, the second 1919-1939, and the third 1946-1958. My intention was to pick up where he left off, considering the history of the League as a whole and focussing on the thirty-four years between 1958 and 1992, the period from publication of *Sixty Seasons* to the formation of the Premier League. Interviews with fans and players from these years illustrate many of the themes I cover in the text. In updating Churchill's study to the fourth and final period of the League, I hope to relate the major events, over those decades, that changed the face of English football for ever.

# Structure of the Football League

The Football League in England grew from a single division in 1888, comprising its twelve founder members, to gradually accommodate ninety-two clubs in four divisions, with amendments made over time to the systems of promotion and relegation within the League. It may be helpful to summarise these here, as reference is made to the structure at different points in time.

1888-91 – Twelve Clubs
1891-92 – Fourteen Clubs
***1892: Second Division Introduced***
1892-93 – Twenty-Eight Clubs: Division One (16); Division Two (12)
1893-94 – Thirty-One Clubs: Division One (16); Division Two (15)
1894-98 – Thirty-Two Clubs: Division One (16); Division Two (16)
1898: Automatic promotion and relegation of two clubs introduced
1898-1905 – Thirty-Six Clubs: Division One (18); Division Two (18)
1905-15 – Forty Clubs: Division One (20); Division Two (20)
1919-20 – Forty-Four Clubs: Division One (22); Division Two (22)
***1920: Third Division Introduced***
1920-21 – Sixty-Six Clubs: Division One (22); Division Two (22); Division Three (22)
***1921: Third Division split into North and South sections;*** one team from each division promoted to the Second Division, with the two relegated clubs being assigned to the more appropriate Third Division

1921-23 – Eighty-Six Clubs: Division One (22); Division Two (22); Division Three North (20); Division Three South (22)
1923-50 – Eighty-Eight Clubs: Division One (22); Division Two (22); Division Three North (22); Division Three South (22)
1950-58 – Ninety-Two Clubs: Division One (22); Division Two (22); Division Three North (24); Division Three South (24)
***1958: Third Divisions North and South re-organised into Divisions Three and Four,*** with no geographical split; four clubs were relegated from Division Three, and four promoted from Division Four
1973: Automatic promotion and relegation of three clubs introduced for Divisions One to Three
***1992: The FA Premier League was formed,*** taking the 22 clubs that would have formed Division One for 1992/93. The remaining three divisions were re-named Division One, Two and Three with the name 'Division Four' disappearing
2004: The lower three divisions were re-named, with Division One becoming the Championship, Division Two becoming League One and Division Three becoming League Two

***Re-election:*** During the first five seasons of league football (until the 1893/94 season), the clubs which finished in the bottom four of the League had to apply for re-election. From the 1894/95 season until 1920/21, the re-election process was required of the clubs which finished in the bottom three of the League. From 1922/23 onwards, it was required of the bottom two teams of both the Third Division North and Third Division South. Since the Fourth Division was established on the eve of the 1958/59 season, the re-election process concerned the bottom four clubs in that division.

Hartlepool United survived re-election a record 14 times between 1924 and 1984, while Southport was the last club to be voted out of the League in 1978. Long recognised as a flawed system, re-election was finally abolished in 1986/87. It was replaced by the automatic relegation of the bottom team in Division Four, with the winners of the Football Conference being promoted (dependent on their stadium meeting the set criteria for membership of the Football League). Promotion and relegation to the Football League was expanded to two clubs in 2003.

## THE GROWTH OF THE FOOTBALL LEAGUE

| Football League | Div 1 | Div 2 | Div 3 (N) | Div 3 (S) | Total |
|---|---|---|---|---|---|
| 1888-91 | 12 | | | | 12 |
| 1891-92 | 14 | | | | 14 |
| 1892-93 | 16 | 12 | | | 28 |
| 1893-94 | 16 | 15 | | | 31 |
| 1894-98 | 16 | 16 | | | 32 |
| 1898-1905 | 18 | 18 | | | 36 |
| 1905-15 | 20 | 20 | | | 40 |
| 1919-20 | 22 | 22 | | | 44 |
| 1920-21 | 22 | 22 | | 22* | 66 |
| 1921-23 | 22 | 22 | 20 | 22 | 86 |
| 1923-50 | 22 | 22 | 22 | 22 | 88 |
| 1950-87 | 22 | 22 | 24** | 24** | 92 |
| 1987-88 | 21 | 23 | 24 | 24 | 92 |
| 1988-91 | 20 | 24 | 24 | 24 | 92 |
| 1991-92 | 22 | 24 | 24 | 22 | 92 |

\*   Division 3
\*\* In 1958, Divisions 3 (N & S) were re-formed as Divisions 3 & 4

# An Overview of the First Sixty Seasons of League Football

The Football Association, itself the oldest football association in the world, was established in 1863 to codify the laws of the game and to oversee and regulate all games in British territory. The FA Cup followed eight years later, and clubs organised their own friendly fixtures, but operated "in a more or less casual, haphazard way."[5] It was not until professionalism was legalised in 1885 that a league system became possible. The origins of the Football League lie with Aston Villa club President William McGregor, who suggested "that ten or twelve of the most prominent clubs in England combine to arrange home-and-away fixtures each season." At a series of meetings, the composition of the League was established, exclusively from the north and midlands, with twelve clubs kicking off the first season in September 1888. The points system of two for a win, and one for a draw was only fixed on 21st November 1888; pitch markings and the rules continued to evolve during those early years. Goal nets and penalty kicks were not introduced until 1891, and the goalkeeper not restricted to handling inside his own area until 1912.

Preston North End, then as now playing at their Deepdale ground, were the early League's dominant team, winning the first two titles. Crowds, initially small, began to grow with general interest in the competition. The League operated a re-election process, voted on by the clubs themselves, which resulted in the first change in the League's composition in 1891, when Sunderland replaced Stoke.

---

5 *The Story of The Football League*: An Official History Published in Commemoration of the Fiftieth Anniversary of its Formation (The Football League, Preston, 1938)

A Second Division was established in 1892, but automatic promotion and relegation did not follow; until 1897/98 a series of 'test matches' took place at the end of the season between the bottom clubs of the First Division and the top of the Second. These fixtures were only abandoned when it was suspected that results were being 'arranged,' and after this the automatic relegation and promotion system was introduced, with two clubs moving between each division.

After Preston, the strongest teams of the early years included Aston Villa in the 1890s, and Newcastle United in the first decade of the twentieth century, while Everton, Sunderland, both Sheffield clubs, Liverpool and Manchester United had all won their first championship titles within 20 years of the League's founding. In the formative period there were a number of short-lived League clubs including Glossop North End, Middlesbrough Ironopolis and New Brighton Tower; other clubs enjoyed a season or two in the League and continue to this day in the non-league system, teams such as Northwich Victoria and Stalybridge Celtic. The League's regional imbalance was mitigated by the arrival of, firstly, Woolwich Arsenal in 1893, followed by Luton Town, Bristol City, Chelsea, Leyton Orient and Tottenham Hotspur, though southern clubs remained in the minority until the end of the First World War.

In 1893 the maximum wage payable to any player was restricted by the League to £140 per year, with 'optional' payments during the close season not to exceed £1 per week. The maximum wage remained a problematic issue for the League until its eventual abolition; it was set at £4 a week (in season) in 1901, rising to £5 in 1910; by 1920, up to £9 only to be reduced back to £8 (£6 in the summer months) two years later. It took until 1947 for the players to secure another increase, to £12 per week (for players with five years unbroken service), and that remained in place for a decade.

On resuming after the First World War, the League took another major step toward expansion with the creation of a Third Division in 1920, filled by clubs from the Southern League, then introduced two separate regional Third Divisions the following year. The game's national status was confirmed when the FA Cup Final first took place at Wembley in 1923. The newly-built Empire Stadium saw a record crowd, unofficially estimated at 300,000; the pitch had to be cleared by mounted police. Crowds began to grow across the country and the inter-war era was a golden age for goalscoring, after the offside law was revised in 1925. The exploits of strikers such as Dixie Dean, George Camsell, Ted Drake and Jimmy Dunne saw records set which stand to this day.

The 1920s saw the emergence of the team manager as a key figure, primarily in the person of Herbert Chapman, "perhaps the greatest manager the league has ever known," according to Churchill. Chapman had overturned a lifetime ban for his involvement in scandal at Leeds City, who were expelled from the League for financial irregularities in 1919. He went on to enjoy great success, firstly at Huddersfield Town and then at Arsenal, before his premature death in 1934. He made tactical innovations and gave an unprecedented attention to fitness and preparation; Chapman was also ahead of his time in proposing European competition and floodlights, in addition to experimenting with shirt numbering, the latter being formally introduced in 1939.

\*\*\*

International football in the British Isles officially began with the meeting of England and Scotland in 1872; not until a tour of Central Europe in 1908 did England play overseas opposition, with Continental fixtures following sporadically over the pre-war decades. The Football Association initially supported domestic clubs to tour both Europe and South America, encouraging the spread of the game in the early twentieth century. There were also a number of British coach/managers operating abroad, notably Jackie Tait Robertson, William Garbutt and Jimmy Hogan, who worked extensively in Europe from before the First World War until the mid-1930s. Hogan is credited with laying down a coaching primer, together with the Austrian Hugo Meisl, which shaped the development of football in Central Europe.

The FA, however, chose to shun the early World Cups with England first entering for the 1950 competition (when they suffered a humiliating 1-0 defeat to the USA), twenty years after the inaugural tournament was held in Uruguay. A famous 6-3 friendly defeat at Wembley to the great Hungary team led by Ferenc Puskás in 1953 was the catalyst which gradually brought an end to English football's insularity and assumption of superiority. The isolationist attitude which had persisted for several decades among the domestic game's hierarchy, and undoubtedly hindered England's development at both club and international level, was crystallised in a statement by FA Member (and future League President) Charles Sutcliffe in 1928:

> "FIFA does not appeal to me... an organisation where such football associations as Uruguay and Paraguay, Brazil and Egypt, Bohemia and Pan Russia are co-equal with England, Scotland, Wales and Ireland seems to me to be a case of magnifying the midgets..."

The visit of Moscow Dynamo on a friendly tour in 1946 gave an insight into the advances made in the world game during England's international isolation; within ten years the leading English clubs were playing in European competition.

The post-Second World War years saw the League's attendances rocket, peaking in 1948/49 but remaining consistently high for another decade. Portsmouth and Wolves (led by Billy Wright, the first man to make 100 appearances for his country) both enjoyed their greatest successes in the post-war era, while Manchester United won three League titles in the 1950s with an exciting young team. 1956, which brought the first Football League match played under floodlights, also saw Stanley Matthews, hero of the 1953 FA Cup Final, win the inaugural European Footballer of the Year award (the Ballon d'Or), reward for his long and distinguished service with Stoke City, Blackpool and England. It was also recognition that, together with the introduction of European club competition, the game's horizons were expanding and becoming increasingly global with the availability of air travel and live television broadcasts. Yet there was continuity with the rich heritage of the past; 1958 marked sixty seasons of League football with consolidation in the form of four national divisions containing 92 clubs – a structure which remained intact until 1992.

# Timeline

**Pre-Second World War:**
1885 – Professionalism legalised
1888 – Football League founded
1891 – Goal nets introduced; Penalty kicks introduced
1893 – Promotion and relegation introduced
1905 – First £1,000 transfer: Alf Common, Sunderland to Middlesbrough
1919 – Leeds City expelled from the Football League for financial irregularities
1925 – New offside law
1928 – First £10,000 transfer: David Jack, Bolton Wanderers to Arsenal
1931 – Wigan Borough became the first club to resign from the League mid-season
1938 – Laws of the Game re-written by FA Secretary Stanley Rous
1939 – Compulsory shirt numbering of players in the League

**Post-Second World War:**
1947 – First £20,000 transfer: Tommy Lawton, Chelsea to Notts County
1951 – White ball introduced
1955 – BBC *Sports Special* highlights first screened, 10th September
1956 – First floodlit League fixture: Portsmouth v Newcastle, 22nd February
1960 – First live televised League fixture: Blackpool v Bolton (ITV), 10th September
1960 – League Cup introduced
1961 – Abolition of maximum wage
1961 – Johnny Haynes of Fulham became the first player paid £100 a week
1961 – First £100,000 transfer involving British club: Denis Law, Manchester City to Torino
1962 – First £100,000 transfer fee paid by British club: Denis Law, Torino to Manchester United
1962 – Accrington Stanley became the second club to resign from the League mid-season
1963 – 'Retain and transfer' system ruled illegal in High Court

1964 – *Match of the Day* first screened on the BBC, 22nd August
1965 – First League Substitute: Keith Peacock, Charlton v Bolton, 21st August
1966 – Substitution allowed for any reason, not just injury
1966 – First £100,000 transfer between British clubs: Alan Ball, Blackpool to Everton
1968 – First England player sent off: Alan Mullery v Yugoslavia, 5th June
1973 – Introduction of three-up, three-down for promotion and relegation
1974 – First League fixture on a Sunday: Millwall v Fulham, 20th January
1976 – Goal difference replaces goal average when clubs equal on points
1976 – First League red card: David Wagstaffe, Blackburn v Leyton Orient, 2nd October
1978 – Effective ban on foreign players lifted by European Union
1978 – First black player to represent England: Viv Anderson v Czechoslovakia, 28th November
1979 – First £1,000,000 transfer between British clubs: Trevor Francis, Birmingham to Nottingham Forest
1981 – Introduction of three points for a win (for 1981-82 season)
1982 – League Cup first sponsored
1983 – Football League first sponsored
1983 – Live televised fixtures resume [see 1960]: Tottenham v Nottingham Forest (ITV), Sun 2nd October; Manchester United v Tottenham (BBC), Fri 16th December
1986 – Introduction of play-offs; promotion/relegation from Football League (for 1986/87 season)
1986 – First £2,000,000 transfers involving British players: Mark Hughes, Manchester United to Barcelona, £2.3m; Gary Lineker, Everton to Barcelona, £2.75m
1987 – Two substitutes allowed for League games
1987 – First £3,000,000 transfer involving British player: Ian Rush, Liverpool to Juventus, £3.2m
1988 – Football League Centenary

1988 – First re-location of Football League club since Southend United in 1955: Scunthorpe United move from the Old Show Ground to Glanford Park
1988 – First £2,000,000 transfer between British clubs: Paul Gascoigne, Newcastle to Tottenham
1989 – Football League and ITV deal for 'live' matches: £44m over 4 years
1989 – First £4,000,000 transfer involving British player: Chris Waddle, Tottenham to Marseille, £4.25m
1991 – First £5,000,000 transfer involving British player: David Platt, Aston Villa to Bari, £5.5m
1992 – First Division (22 clubs) breakaway to become FA Premier League. Football League left with 3 divisions (70 clubs)

## From Churchill to the 1960s

"The Football League thought that the maximum wage was fundamental to healthy competition. If it were abolished, they argued, the good players would go to a few clubs, the money would go to a few players and the rest would starve." Ward & Williams, *Football Nation: Sixty Years of the Beautiful Game*

The 1960s began with a significant development, which has reverberated through the English game ever since – the abolition of professional football's historic maximum wage. At the Football League's Annual General Meeting of June 1957, it was fixed at £20 a week during the season (equivalent to approximately £493 in 2020), which reduced to £17 over the summer. The campaign to abolish the wage restriction was spearheaded by Fulham player Jimmy Hill, leader of the players' union, the Professional Footballers' Association (PFA), which had threatened to strike. His argument was that "the players should be paid the maximum that clubs can afford to pay them," and should be granted "the freedom to earn as much as they can negotiate with their employers. There should be no artificial ceiling."

Hill had taken over union leadership in 1957 from Jimmy Guthrie, an ex-Dundee and Portsmouth player who advocated an "aggressive, radical, high-profile stance." Firstly, the name was changed from the Association Football Players' and Trainers' Union to the PFA and then, in 1960, under Hill it "formulated four principal demands: abolition of the maximum wage, the right of players to a proportion of their transfer fees, a new retaining system and new contracts."[6]

6 David Russell, *Football and the English: a social history of association football in England, 1863-1995* (1997)

The threat of strike action during 1960/61 was given weight by the support of star players including Stanley Matthews, English football's biggest name, which forced the clubs' hand. The League agreed to meet the bulk of the PFA's demands at their June 1961 Annual General Meeting, primarily the abolition of the maximum wage.

Though conceding to the players on wages, the League fought against the removal of the 'retain and transfer' system, a legacy of the Victorian era which allowed a club to hold a player's license, thus preventing him from transferring to another club unless it was beneficial for them. It was an arrangement that, as Football League Secretary Alan Hardaker confessed, "enabled a club to retain a player against his will at the end of his contract and, not only that, to pay him less money while doing so." After a lengthy legal challenge initiated by the England international George Eastham, the archaic system of 'retain and transfer,' having lasted until 1963, was overturned by Mr Justice Wilberforce in the High Court as "an unjustifiable restraint of trade." Full freedom of contract was however not established for another fifteen years. Eastham, who wished to leave Newcastle United, had stopped playing and had taken up a job as a salesman after having three transfer requests turned down, though Newcastle eventually relented and sold him to Arsenal in November 1960.

The result of these two judgements, as Arthur Hopcraft observed, "marked the end of the total dominance of the game's boardrooms over the players," and made "every professional player a free agent... able to negotiate his pay and his length of service with a club." Over the subsequent decades, it became apparent that, taken together, they also "set the Football League on an organic trajectory of development," in a spiral of rising wages and uneven wealth re-distribution which led eventually to the crises of the 1980s and the formation of the 'breakaway' Premier League. As Tony Arnold[7] noted, those "controls on players' wages and mobility (the retain and transfer system) were important influences until the 1960s on the equalisation of playing standards between clubs, particularly 'city' and 'town' clubs with different audience potentials."

7 Tony Arnold, 'Rich man, poor man: the Football League' in *British Football and Social Change* (ed. John Williams and Stephen Wagg, 1991)

Though the players benefitted immediately, with Hill's Fulham teammate Johnny Haynes becoming the first player to command a £100-a-week wage in 1961, this is widely viewed in retrospect as the moment from which competition within the Football League was to become steadily less equal.

Hopcraft articulated fears about "a Super League, in which all the leading European clubs would play, breaking away from the domestic leagues in their own countries," as early as the 1960s. Though he was sceptical about that prospect, he believed "a more likely suggestion is that a domestic Premier League may hive off from the English Football League to confine top-quality football to perhaps a dozen of the country's major areas of population." *The Daily Mirror's* chief football writer Frank McGhee felt that the movement of players to the bigger clubs in the wake of the lifting of the maximum wage "is an indication that the day of the Super League is nearer. The day when all the top talent in the country is concentrated in, perhaps, a dozen clubs. And it will be a great thing for English football." Another journalist, David Miller of *The Times*, also predicted the emergence of a Super League, arguing in 1963 that the PFA's victory two years earlier "succeeded primarily in putting much money into the hands of a relatively few players."

The seismic effects of the changes to transfers and wages were not fully apparent initially, for the League's democratic share of resources was reflected in championships won by eight different clubs over the 1960s, a decade preceded by Wolverhampton Wanderers' 1958/59 triumph. Champions included provincial sides such as Burnley and Ipswich Town, who won the League title in their very first season in the top division, 1961/62, a unique feat. Both Leyton Orient and Northampton Town enjoyed their first (and, to date, only) seasons in the First Division during the decade. However, bigger-city clubs, notably Leeds United and Liverpool, who had been languishing in the Second Division at the start of the decade, began to establish themselves as major forces, both winning the League soon after promotion. Their success was due in large part to their hugely influential and revered managers, Don Revie at Leeds and Liverpool's Bill Shankly, "a Scottish socialist who believed in socialist football – keep the game simple, work hard for each other and share the load for the greater good. He was pleased that Liverpool wore red shirts and he thought that all players in the team should be paid the same wages."[8]

The triumvirate of great managers was made up by Manchester United's Matt Busby, another Scot who, in addition to winning two League titles and fielding the celebrated attack of George Best, Bobby Charlton and Denis Law (all three were voted European Footballer of the Year during the decade), secured the first-ever European Champions' Cup win by an English club in 1968 – although Glasgow's Celtic had triumphed a year earlier. It was a poignant triumph for Manchester United, coming a decade after 'Busby's Babes' were lost in the Munich air crash of 1958, and especially fitting as Busby had been a strong advocate of competing in Europe at a time of opposition from the League. "Challenges," he said, "should be met, not avoided."

It was Gabriel Hanot, editor of the French daily sports paper *L'Equipe,* who had first championed the idea of a European club tournament, partly in response to the claim of Wolves manager Stan Cullis, after victories in friendly matches over Moscow Spartak and Honved in 1954, that his side were "The champions of the world." The Football League initially resisted, requesting Chelsea withdraw from the inaugural European Champions' Cup in 1955, but it was soon acceptable for clubs to play in Europe alongside domestic competition; the influence of Continental football accordingly grew throughout the 1960s. The exposure to different playing styles arguably increased tactical awareness and resulted in technical innovations in the English game, demonstrated first by the successes of Tottenham Hotspur and West Ham United in the European Cup Winners' Cup, and then Leeds United, Newcastle United, Arsenal (all in the third European competition, the Fairs Cup), Manchester City, and Chelsea at the end of the decade.

\*\*\*

---

8 Andrew Ward and John Williams, *Football Nation: Sixty Years of the Beautiful Game* (2009)

The League had a number of star players in Gordon Banks, Danny Blanchflower, Bobby Charlton, Bobby Moore, John Charles, Jimmy Greaves, and Denis Law; the latter three all transferred to Italian clubs for large sums, with Law commanding the first £100,000 fee. Footballers playing abroad enjoyed varying degrees of success; while Charles and Gerry Hitchens thrived in Italy, Greaves and Law never settled, and they both returned to English football within a year. The growth of European competition and the export of players were among the early signs of globalisation and international influences which would eventually come to define England's top division.

The first modern superstar was George Best of Manchester United and Northern Ireland, a phenomenal player in an era of poor pitches and often brutal tackling, who became a celebrity beyond football. When Derrick Collier, hailing him as Footballer of the Year in 1968, stated, "There has never been a man like George Best – footballer and successful business tycoon",[9] it was no exaggeration. Noting that Best is "Sophisticated, though in the manner of this day and age, he likes clothes – modern gear – drives fast sleek cars and enjoys himself in the thoroughly modern manner", Collier speculates, "Perhaps it can be said that this footballer, who runs his own rapidly expanding fan-club, will be the first man of his profession to make a cool million."

In his heyday, Best was pictured with actors, fashion models and pop stars, designed and modelled clothes, and even co-owned a Manchester boutique, Edwardia, with Manchester City's Mike Summerbee. By 1969, it was reckoned that over half of Best's income came from his commercial contracts, while his basic salary at Manchester United was between £5-6,000 a year. Although he enjoyed great fame, and continues to be synonymous with the game even among non-football fans, Best's wealth was moderate when considered by current standards. Despite great early success as part of Manchester United's League and European Cup-winning teams of the late sixties, he was in decline by his mid-twenties, and left Old Trafford in 1974, at 27, spending the rest of his career in short spells at various clubs around the world.

---

[9] Writing in *The Park Drive Book of Football* (1968)

He said of his career: "I spent a lot of money on booze, birds and fast cars – the rest I just squandered."

With English clubs competing in, and winning, their first European trophies, the national team too grew in stature. Alf Ramsey, who had guided Ipswich Town to their 1962 League title, was appointed England manager in 1963, and set about professionalising the set-up, insisting on complete control where previously, squad and team selection were made by committee, often over the head of the nominal manager. Described as "obstinate, a cunning tactician and single-minded in his pursuit of success", Ramsey brought an astute, even ruthless, management style to the national team. He demonstrated that he was not afraid to make unpopular decisions when discarding wingers, regarded as the key to scoring goals in English football. Aided by home advantage and a crop of highly talented players, Ramsey guided England to success at the 1966 World Cup, a triumph which gave the domestic game a huge, if short-lived, boost.

\*\*\*

The steady decline in both attendances and goals became English football's main preoccupation from the 1950s onward; both were to become more acute in the years that followed the 1966 World Cup victory. Smaller crowds were the result of developments in wider society, primarily the broadening scope of entertainment and leisure options as an alternative to attending matches. Arnold attributed the falling attendances, which never regained their peak of 1949, to economic and social changes, specifically "increases in disposable incomes, in leisure time, and in personal mobility", with competing attractions reducing football's virtual monopoly on the immediate post-war leisure market. Bryon Butler[10] likewise noted that, by the 1960s, attendances reflected societal changes, namely "a more affluent society with cars, television and many more affordable options to fill its leisure hours." Among the first casualties of the squeezed finances for smaller clubs were Accrington Stanley, when they were forced to resign from the Football League in March 1962.

10 Bryon Butler, *The Official Illustrated History of the Football League* (1987)

In response, League Secretary Alan Hardaker proposed a 'Pattern for Football' in 1963, including a re-structuring to five twenty-club divisions (a return to the former regionalisation model at the bottom of the League) and 'four up, four down' promotion and relegation, which was promptly rejected. Hardaker, together with the League's President, fellow Yorkshireman Joe Richards, had introduced the League Cup competition in 1960 (with a trophy Richards purchased himself) as a new source of income, but was increasingly convinced that clubs were acting in their own interests rather than for the collective benefit of the Football League.

David Russell[11] records that, by the middle of the sixties, it was apparent that "goal-scoring levels were never again to reach those of the period 1955-62. In this sense, the game had changed for good." The steady decline in goals throughout the League reflected the changing nature of the game itself, an evolution partly due to the greater fitness of players, who benefitted from more scientific training methods, and an increased attention to conditioning and diet. The introduction of a substitute in 1965 (before then, teams who lost a player had to simply re-organise themselves and play on with ten men) added another option for managers. Though substitutes were initially to be used strictly as a replacement for an injured player, that rule was relaxed within two years, due to alleged gamesmanship on the part of certain clubs and managers, whose players suffered 'injuries' at convenient moments. However, not until 1987 was a second substitute permitted in the Football League, so that an injury or sending-off early in a game often determined its outcome, a like-for-like replacement being only a matter of chance.

The increased emphasis on physical conditioning coincided with the introduction of sophisticated defensive systems and greater tactical awareness, often influenced by exposure to the methods of overseas sides in club or international competition. England's humiliation at the hands of Hungary in 1953, and the participation of the top sides in European tournaments from the late 1950s, brought recognition that changes in the style of English football were inevitable. The combined effects created a

---

11 David Russell, *Football and the English: a social history of association football in England, 1863-1995* (1997)

different kind of game than the free-scoring, all-out attacking of earlier eras, one where defensive shape and the denying of space to opponents became integral. It became the norm for teams to adopt a more negative approach when playing away from home. The *FA Yearbook* of 1959/60 was possibly the first to announce the coming of the age of "gamesmanship, the art of cheating fairly" to English football. Russell further observed that:

> "From the late 1950s there was much discussion of the 'spirit' in which the game was being played. Many observers claimed that, as financial rewards rose, so players became more 'cynical,' more prone to challenge referees, to waste time, steal distance at free kicks and indulge in deliberate petty fouling. The decline in goal-scoring was also often cited as evidence for their case by those arguing that the game had lost direction."

So it was that in June 1966, a month before England's World Cup victory, sufficient concerns about the general state of the game remained for Harold Wilson's Labour government to commission a wide-ranging report. Headed by Norman Chester, a political economist and Warden of Nuffield College, Oxford University, the investigating committee had input from figures inside and outside professional football,[12] and its terms of reference were:

> "To enquire into the state of Association Football at all levels, including the organisation, management, finance and administration, and the means by which the game may be developed for the public good; and to make recommendations"

Under this broad remit, the first Chester Report considered the finances of football, the condition of stadia, the impact of television, the dominance of big-city teams, transfer fees, and behaviour and discipline on and off the field. Published in 1968, it noted substantial losses in the lower three divisions and surpluses at the top, concluding that "there is no need to create a

---

[12] The Committee of 11 included M.P.'s, a Q.C. and a Justice of the Peace, an economist and an industrialist, an ex-footballer and a referee.

super league, it already exists in the top clubs of the First Division."

Among its recommendations was a re-structuring of the League and a return to the regionalisation of the bottom divisions. Observing, "we do not think it would be good for the game or the players if transfer fees continued to rise", the Committee proposed a levy on transfer fees over £25,000, to "be paid by the purchasing club, the proceeds being used by the League for encouraging ground improvements." It looked at the forces "tending to make the rich richer and the poor poorer", with potential solutions including Sunday and summer football, the amalgamation of clubs or at least ground-sharing arrangements, and improved facilities at stadiums.

On the subject of player discipline, the Report stated, "the situation is to be deplored. Dirty play reduces the stature of the game for players and spectators alike. If it occurs in a match which appears on television it presents the game in a very bad light to millions of people." It further "found the querying of the referee's decision to be a particularly distasteful aspect of football not found in rugby or other sports." Its recommendation was that only team captains should be allowed to approach the referee during a game. As for crowd trouble, "an increase in disorderly behaviour by spectators" was recorded, and it was suggested that clubs be either heavily fined or have their ground temporarily closed as a result. On the vexed question of television, while accepting it could become an important source of revenue, the Chester Report ominously noted that the "mass use of television is likely to widen the gap between the top and the bottom clubs."

Discussed in Parliament in 1969, MPs observed that football was now "big business", with "a tremendous impact on the life of the country." The issues raised in this first Chester Report were only to become more pressing over the following years, and football had not heard the last of Norman Chester.

# The Transfer Market (Part One)

The problem of the 'poaching' of players registered with another club was evident from the League's earliest days, and was addressed by its Management Committee in 1890: "any League club offering inducements to a player of another League club to leave the club... shall be deemed guilty of objectionable conduct." Yet then, as now, clubs and players often found a way around the official regulations, despite the League issuing fines and further legislating to limit any signing-on fee to £10. The League did impose sanctions where its regulations were breached; this led to Aston Villa being forced to pay West Bromwich Albion £100 in 1893 for the services of Willie Groves, one of the many Scots plying his trade in the Football League. Villa were also fined after being accused of poaching Groves and team-mate Jack Reynolds.

The practice of 'borrowing' players was another scourge of the formative years, which the League formally banned in April 1898, but it persisted unofficially over the years; not until 1966 was the loan system introduced to permit temporary signings.

The first £1,000 transfer was that of Alf Common, from Sunderland to Middlesbrough on Valentine's Day, February 14th, 1905. The furore caused by Common's signing led to an FA enquiry, questions being raised in the House of Commons, and criticism of both clubs for engaging in what was described as "a new type of white slave trade." In 1908, a proposal to limit transfer fees to £350 was discussed but, with the League reluctant to legislate, "it was easily broken through, and lasted only four months."[13] In the years before the First World War, Blackburn Rovers, under Chairman and benefactor Lawrence

---

13 *The Story of The Football League*: An Official History Published in Commemoration of the Fiftieth Anniversary of its Formation (The Football League, Preston, 1938)

Cotton, were the League's big spenders, setting three new record fees in as many years, two of them signings from Scotland.

A transfer which reversed the historical trend of Scots moving to the English league was the signing of West Ham's Syd Puddefoot by Scottish club Falkirk in February 1922; a world record of £5,000 at the time, Puddefoot's fee was raised with the help of supporter subscriptions, and prompted the *Football Post* to ask "When will this folly on the part of football clubs come to an end?" That record was short-lived, as England full-back Warney Cresswell moved from South Shields to Sunderland for £5,500 the very next month, and was broken again in 1925 when the same club bought Bob Kelly for £6,500 from Burnley. 1922, the year of Puddefoot's landmark move, also saw Arsenal make a proposal that "the maximum sum which shall be paid or received in respect of one player shall be £1,650." After that attempt to limit fees was, once more, rejected, "prices tended to soar to hitherto unimagined heights, and it is significant of the effect of the clubs' attitude that the Arsenal itself was amongst those which paid much increased sums for the players they wanted."[14]

Arsenal established a reputation as the 'Bank of England club' as they spent heavily and enjoyed great success under manager Herbert Chapman in the late 1920s and early 1930s. With increased revenue from large crowds at Highbury, North London, where they had moved from Woolwich in 1913, Chairman Sir Henry Norris sanctioned the spending spree. Charles Buchan, an England international, and Scottish goalkeeper William Harper had already been expensively signed before they paid the world's first five-figure sum for Bolton's David Jack in 1928. Chapman is reputed to have engineered the transfer at a hotel bar, plying Bolton's representatives with alcohol while he remained sober, and securing the player for what he believed to be a bargain price. The FA's President, Sir Charles Clegg, was unimpressed, declaring that no player in the world was worth that sum. Alex James from Preston was another big signing in 1929, and after Chapman's death the club was still prepared to pay record fees, bringing Welsh international Bryn Jones from rivals Wolves in 1938 for £14,500.

14 *The Story of The Football League*, ibid.

When League football resumed after the Second World War, another landmark fee soon followed, as in 1947 Tommy Lawton was the subject of the first £20,000 transfer. Lawton leaving Chelsea for Notts County was something of a sensation, a current England international in his prime moving from the First Division to the Third. With wages capped at £12 a week, he explained that the transfer "had assured the future of my wife and daughter", as County had arranged for him to join "a famous typewriting firm, with whom I am now learning the business, and where I hope to have a long and successful career when my soccer days are over."[15]

Sunderland broke the transfer record twice more, firstly to bring Len Shackleton from Newcastle only months after Lawton's move, and then making Trevor Ford the first £30,000 footballer when he signed from Aston Villa in 1950. The following decade saw Italian clubs, who had been importing footballers from around the world since the late 1920s, sign a succession of Football League players for record fees: Eddie Firmani (1955), John Charles (1957), Gerry Hitchens (1961), and then Denis Law, already transferred from Huddersfield to Manchester City for a domestic record £55,000 in 1960, moved to Torino for double that fee a year later. When Law returned to England with Manchester United in 1962, at £115,000 it was the first time a British club had paid a six-figure sum.

After the maximum wage was abolished in 1961, there were renewed fears of an explosion in transfer fees. 1967 was "a boom year with over £4m changing hands in the transfer market"[16] and, the following year, a £125,000 deal taking Martin Chivers from Southampton to Spurs came under scrutiny. The fee was described by League President Len Shipman (also Chairman of Leicester City) as "too ridiculous for words." He threatened that the League "would have to look into the matter", and related that he had "been talking recently to a club director who visualises fees reaching £250,000 within the next six years." Before that sum was reached, another England forward, Allan Clarke, was twice transferred for British record fees, from Fulham to Leicester in 1968 and again onto Leeds the following year.

15 Tommy Lawton, *Football is my Business* (1948)
16 *The Manchester United Book of Football No. 3* (1968)

The 1968 Chester Report had recommended a levy on transfer fees above £25,000 in order to check the inflation of the market. While urging the implementation of many of its recommendations, Minister for Sport Denis Howell rejected the suggestion of the transfer fee levy. He did however concede "that where these big transfer fees are paid, some of that money ought to go back into the game as a whole, for the good of the game."

Although there was no official limit, for many decades fees were kept in check by the limited finances available to clubs, with their only revenue generated by attendances. Long before super-rich owners, television income and sponsorship deals, clubs were forced to live within their means, and spend accordingly. The historical emphasis for the best part of a hundred years, even at the highest level of the Football League, remained on clubs finding and developing their own talent. Most used scouting networks to identify players, not only locally, but drawn from across the British Isles. Matt Busby at Manchester United was prepared to break the transfer record to bring Denis Law back from Italy, but youth development was the club's trademark. Scouts Louis Rocca and Joe Armstrong played a major part in Manchester United's early history and, having already built the young side which was tragically destroyed in the Munich air crash, Busby was able to find players such as George Best, discovered by Northern Ireland-based scout Bob Bishop.

The pattern was repeated around the League; Wally St Pier, West Ham's legendary scout, brought future World Cup winners Geoff Hurst, Bobby Moore and Martin Peters to the club as schoolboys, among many others. Liverpool, under Bill Shankly and later Bob Paisley, created and made full use of a network led by Chief Scout Geoff Twentyman to identify young players at lower-league clubs, many of whom became internationals, including Kevin Keegan, Ray Clemence, Phil Neal, and Ian Rush. This model also maintained the tradition of transfer fees re-distributing wealth from the top throughout the divisions of the Football League.

## Progress of British Transfer Record (1888-1960)

| | | |
|---|---|---|
| Sep 1893 | Willie Groves (West Brom-Aston Villa) | £100 |
| Jan 1904 | Andy McCombie (Sunderland-Newcastle) | £700 |
| Feb 1905 | Alf Common (Sunderland-Middlesbrough) | £1,000 |
| Feb 1911 | John Simpson (Falkirk-Blackburn) | £1,800 |
| Jan 1913 | Danny Shea (West Ham-Blackburn) | £2,000 |
| Feb 1914 | Percy Dawson (Hearts-Blackburn) | £2,500 |
| Dec 1920 | David Mercer (Hull-Sheffield U) | £4,500 |
| Feb 1922 | Syd Puddefoot (West Ham-Falkirk) | £5,000 |
| Mar 1922 | Warney Cresswell (S Shields-Sunderland) | £5,500 |
| Dec 1925 | Bob Kelly (Burnley-Sunderland) | £6,500 |
| Apr 1927 | James Gibson (Partick-Aston Villa) | £7,500 |
| Oct 1928 | David Jack (Bolton-Arsenal) | £10,890 |
| Mar 1938 | Bryn Jones (Wolves-Arsenal) | £14,500 |
| Sep 1947 | Billy Steel (Morton-Derby) | £15,500 |
| Nov 1947 | Tommy Lawton (Chelsea-Notts County) | £20,000 |
| Feb 1948 | Len Shackleton (Newcastle-Sunderland) | £20,500 |
| Feb 1949 | Johnny Morris (Manchester U-Derby) | £24,000 |
| Dec 1949 | Eddie Quigley (Sheffield W-Preston) | £26,500 |
| Oct 1950 | Trevor Ford (Aston Villa-Sunderland) | £30,000 |
| Mar 1951 | Jackie Sewell (Notts County-Sheffield W) | £34,500 |
| Jul 1955 | Eddie Firmani (Charlton-Sampdoria) | £35,000 |
| Apr 1957 | John Charles (Leeds-Juventus) | £65,000 |

# The 1970s

"High admission prices, the prima-donna attitudes of some of our players, violence on the terraces and a lack of entertainment are all contributory factors in a general problem." Danny Williams, Mansfield Town manager, in *The Football League Review,* 1972

For all English football's problems on and off the pitch during the 1970s, the First Division remained a highly-competitive power-house with traditional title winners and well-supported big-city clubs challenged by provincial outsiders. To lift the Football League Championship was the domestic game's most coveted honour. Liverpool, under Bill Shankly and his successor Bob Paisley, with star players Kevin Keegan and Kenny Dalglish, were the pre-eminent side with four League titles, but elsewhere honours were shared between Everton, Arsenal, and Don Revie's powerful Leeds United; the decade saw the first titles won by Derby County (twice), and the triumph of Nottingham Forest under Brian Clough. When Forest backed up their league success by winning consecutive European Cups, it reinforced the total dominance of English clubs. Forest's victories were part of the unprecedented six European Cup trophies in a row, from 1977 to 1982, which came to England.

Clough, who was in charge for Derby's 1971/72 title win, became the first manager since Herbert Chapman with Huddersfield Town and Arsenal in the 1930s to guide two different clubs to the League Championship, when his Nottingham Forest side lifted the 1977/78 title, in their first season after promotion from the Second Division. Clough and fellow managers like Malcolm Allison at Manchester City were outspoken figures, in demand for television appearances as pundits and frequently offering controversial opinions.

The continuing democracy of the Football League was reflected in the relegations of major clubs – notably Manchester United in 1974, six years after their historic European Cup triumph, Tottenham Hotspur three years later, Chelsea twice – and the promotion to the top division of such clubs as Bristol City, Brighton, and Carlisle United. Meanwhile, the strength (and depth) of competition was emphasised by the sharing of major honours in the domestic cups. The FA Cup was won by thirteen different teams in the thirteen seasons between 1966 and 1978, and saw three Second Division sides lift the trophy between 1973 and 1980 (when West Ham United became the last lower-division side to win the Cup).

The League Cup, a mid-week competition initially viewed with some suspicion, had become established with a one-off Wembley final in 1967. The added incentive of a European place for the winners, from the 1970/71 season onwards, finally led to all League clubs entering the tournament. This second cup competition also had a variety of winners, from Birmingham City, Norwich City, Leicester City, QPR, and Swindon Town in the 1960s, to Stoke City (their first major trophy), and long-awaited victories for Wolves and Aston Villa in the 1970s.

The 1970s saw the first change in the system of promotion and relegation for nearly 80 years. Three clubs up and three down, instead of two, came into force for the 1973/74 season, allowing for greater mobility within the League, and the involvement of more clubs vying for promotion or to avoid relegation. The League itself retained the system of 're-election,' whereby a vote at the Annual General Meeting determined whether the bottom four teams in the Fourth Division would keep their status, or be replaced by a non-league applicant. There was more movement in the 1970s than previously, with Bradford Park Avenue, Barrow, Workington and Southport all voted out of the League, replaced by Cambridge United, Hereford United, Wimbledon and Wigan Athletic. The results of the ballot did not necessarily follow league placing, and the practice was open to criticism, with the Bradford Park Avenue Chairman Herbert Metcalfe insisting "We have gone out because of the Freemasonry of Football" after his club's demotion. After Southport's demise in 1978 no further clubs were voted out of the League, and re-election was finally abandoned for the 1986/87 season in favour of automatic promotion and relegation.

Where England's 1966 World Cup win gave the domestic game a boost, the ailing fortunes of the national side during the 1970s were a source of angst and much debate. Alf Ramsey arguably took an even stronger squad to defend the title in the 1970 Mexico tournament, only to be undone by West Germany in the quarter-finals. When his ageing side failed to qualify for the 1974 World Cup, he was replaced with Leeds United's successful manager Don Revie. Unfortunately, Revie was unable to replicate his club success at international level and, declaring the job was "no longer worth the aggravation", he controversially resigned in 1977 to take up a post in the United Arab Emirates, with England too far behind in the qualifiers to reach the following year's World Cup. The FA promptly charged Revie with bringing the game into disrepute, and banned him from English football for ten years; the ban was overturned in the High Court, though the judge, Justice Cantley, was scathing about his conduct: "Mr Revie... presented to the public a sensational and notorious example of disloyalty, breach of duty, discourtesy and selfishness." Despite popular support and several trophies, Brian Clough was again overlooked when the FA approached West Ham's Ron Greenwood as Revie's successor. England qualified for the 1980 European Championships and 1982 World Cup under Greenwood.

The failure to qualify for successive World Cups in the decade, despite a wealth of talent in the League, was a source of much soul-searching. England's tradition of goalkeeping excellence was maintained by Gordon Banks and his successor, Peter Shilton, who followed Banks from Leicester to Stoke for a world record fee for a goalkeeper of £325,000 in November 1974. Liverpool's Ray Clemence challenged Shilton for the number one spot toward the end of the 1970s and early 80s, while Manchester City's top-class keeper Joe Corrigan barely got a look-in. However, further up the pitch, lenient referees allowed defenders to stifle creativity with rugged, at times brutal, tackling. Yet even with George Best's decline (largely due to off-field factors), a number of creative players thrived in the First Division, despite the heavy pitches and tough tackling which often went unpunished. The skills of Stan Bowles, Tony

Currie, Alan Hudson and Rodney Marsh were among those to flourish in the First Division, but successive England managers seemed to view their talents as a luxury, and they were sparingly used in the national team; for all their undoubted ability, that quartet won only 33 caps between them.

The League still contained an abundance of talent, confirmed by the fact that the bulk of the Scottish squads who qualified for both the 1974 and 1978 World Cup tournaments were drawn from top First Division teams. The Scottish influence on English football, present from its founding, remained strong throughout the latter years of the Football League. Managers Busby, Shankly and Dave Mackay lifted the title in the 1960s and 70s, while Kenny Dalglish and George Graham dominated the later 1980s; Alex Ferguson, in charge at Manchester United since 1986, then became the most successful manager of the Premier League era. Meanwhile players such as Billy Bremner, Kenny Burns, Dalglish, Archie Gemmill, Peter Lorimer, Frank McLintock, Bruce Rioch and Graeme Souness were influential at the First Division's leading teams. While England struggled in the 70s, Scotland went on to qualify for every World Cup between 1974 and 1990, with the core of their team drawn from the top of the English league.

\*\*\*

The 1970s saw the emergence of a whole generation of black footballers. The history of black players in the Football League dates from Arthur Wharton, a goalkeeper for Darlington, Preston and Rotherham in the very first years of the League, and Walter Tull of Tottenham before the First World War, through to Jamaican Lindy Delapenha in the 1940s and South African Albert Johanneson, who became the first black player to participate in an FA Cup Final, for Leeds United in 1965. However, it was not until April 1972 that an English top-flight team fielded three black players (Clyde Best, Clive Charles and Ade Coker for West Ham United against Tottenham Hotspur). It took several more years for another team to follow suit – West Bromwich Albion in 1979, with the celebrated trio of Brendan Batson, Laurie Cunningham and Cyrille Regis. By then, there were black players throughout the League and, as Emy

Onuora[17] has observed of West Brom's trail-blazing players, "Their presence was no longer an anomaly; this was a movement." Manchester City recruited locally, from Wilbraham High School in Chorlton, "a crop of boys from in and around Moss Side" who reached the first team – Dave and Gary Bennett, Roger Palmer, Alex Williams (the first black goalkeeper to play in the top division of English football, in 1981), and Clive Wilson.

It was unfortunately also a time of troubled race relations, with the National Front and extreme right-wing groups targeting football, and a number of stadiums were notorious for the levels of racist vitriol directed at black players during matches. Batson commented that "What shocked me when I joined West Brom was the volume… The noise and level of the abuse was incredible. At times, it was like surround sound in the grounds. But it was such a regular occurrence, you almost got used to it." In addition to sustained booing and chanting inside the grounds, all three West Brom players received hate mail, some containing death threats, and a bullet was sent in the post to Regis ahead of his England debut.

The ability and success of Viv Anderson, Cunningham and Regis (the first three black players to represent the full England side), plus others throughout the League, including Stan Horne, Johnny Miller, Cliff Marshall, Tunji Banjo, John Chiedozie, Luther Blissett, George Berry, Bob Hazell, Garth Crooks, Vince Hilaire, Ricky Hill, Cec Podd, Trevor Lee and Phil Walker gradually helped to overcome prejudice. Regis was later to say "We inspired the second and third generations. We early players were just the tip of the iceberg. What stopped racism in my mind was more and more teams had black players." Onoura confirmed that "as more and more black footballers became established within their sides, the level of terrace abuse subsided and eventually disappeared altogether at some grounds."

\*\*\*

---

17 Emy Onuora, *Pitch Black: The Story of Black British Footballers* (2015)

From the beginning, the Football League had sought to protect its local, and national, characteristics. For the very first season of the League, in 1888, there was a stipulation that players had to either be born within six miles of the club's ground, or been resident within that area for two years. The regulation did not prevent an influx of Scottish players, at that time regarded as technically superior to their English counterparts. The residence requirement was soon relaxed, and a Canadian of Swiss heritage, Walter Bowman, is credited as being the first foreign national to play in the Football League, for Accrington in 1892. The early league saw even more exotic arrivals in the form of German Max Seeberg, who made a single appearance for Tottenham in the 1908/09 season, and Egyptian Hussein Hegazi who played briefly for Fulham three years later. Chelsea's first foreign player, Dane Nils Middelboe, an amateur who represented his country at three Olympic Games, arrived in 1913; these early imports were of course isolated examples.

An attempt in 1930 by Arsenal manager Herbert Chapman to sign Rudi Hiden, an Austrian goalkeeper, was blocked by the Ministry of Labour in the face of protests by the Football League and Players' Union. Charles Sutcliffe, later to become League President, led the outcry, declaring "The idea of bringing foreigners to play in league football is repulsive to the clubs, offensive to British players and a terrible confession of weakness in the management of a club." Chapman turned instead to a Dutch goalkeeper, Gerry Keizer, who was already resident in the UK and had also played as an amateur. The uproar caused by the Hiden case was the catalyst for formal regulation, in June 1931. This was definitive for the best part of five decades:

> "A professional player who is not a British-born subject is not eligible to take part in any competition under British jurisdiction unless he has a two years' qualification."

While Chilean-born George Robledo and celebrated German goalkeeper Bert Trautmann met the residence requirement (Trautmann by virtue of his time in a prisoner-of-war camp), this naturally limited the number of imports. A few players, including Albert Guðmundsson of Iceland (at Arsenal), Swedes

Dan Ekner (Portsmouth) and Hans Jeppson (Charlton), were contracted as amateurs rather than professionals, an exemption which allowed them a short stay in English football before moving to other European clubs. However, 'British jurisdiction' enabled footballers from the Commonwealth, Jamaican Lindy Delapenha at Portsmouth, South Africans Berry Nieuwenhuys of Liverpool, Steve Mokone (Coventry), Gerry Francis and Albert Johanesson at Leeds, Bermudan Clyde Best and Nigerian Ade Coker at West Ham, plus, briefly, Hong Kong-born Cheung Chi Doy at Blackpool, to play League football.

It was not until 1978 that European Union legislation forced the League to relax its long-standing restrictions on overseas players, with the first arrivals following that summer's World Cup. The high-profile signings of Argentina's winners Ossie Ardiles and Ricky Villa were a sensational coup for Tottenham on 10th July 1978. England manager, Ron Greenwood, congratulated Tottenham "on their enterprise", and believed "It is short-sighted to object to the arrival of someone like Ardiles. His presence can only benefit the English game, show at first hand that skill can triumph in our game." Wider reactions were mixed; Greenwood's enthusiasm was in contrast to the PFA's Cliff Lloyd, who warned "I don't think we would stand for a big influx of Argentinians to this country." Ardiles and Villa were rapidly followed by Alex Sabella and Alberto Tarantini, both Argentines, Ivan Golac of Yugoslavia, Kazimierz Deyna of Poland and Arnold Muhren of the Netherlands. The man who signed Muhren was Bobby Robson, who succeeded Greenwood as England manager in 1982, and another advocate for imports: "I think the advent of foreign players has been a good thing for football in this country and while they continue to have something to offer the game, they'll keep coming in."

Such was the concern that by 31st July, player imports from non-Common Market countries were temporarily banned by the UK government until talks could take place between the Department of Employment and the PFA, which was naturally concerned that its members could be displaced. A compromise was reached to limit overseas players at two per team, and with the proviso that they were 'established performers.' Whilst clubs continued to import players over the subsequent seasons, few had the impact of Ardiles and Villa, or the Dutchmen Muhren and Frans Thijssen at Ipswich; Deyna, Sabella and Tarantini, for example, all struggled, and none remained long in the Football League.

The inevitable problems of adapting to a new climate, culture, and language were often exacerbated on the field. Another Argentine, Claudio Marangoni, who lasted a single season at Sunderland in 1979/80, outlined some of the footballing difficulties facing the new arrivals: "I am trying very hard to adjust and settle to the game in England. It's another kind of football... In Argentina, they always play the ball to feet and they like touch and dribbling. Here, the goalkeeper shoots long balls and you have to fight to get it." Like Sabella, he played in the Second Division, and added "Some of the pitches I have found very difficult to play on since I came here."

Marangoni's experience, echoed by several other foreign players to sample the Football League in this era, was one of the factors which served to curb the flow of imports, at least temporarily. David Russell felt that the combination of regulation and the failure of several early signings, "delayed the mass arrival of the overseas player for another twenty years."[18] Even with the coming of the Premier League, its opening day in August 1992 saw a mere thirteen overseas footballers scattered among the twenty teams, though that was soon to change.

\*\*\*

The Football League also had to contend with domestic players looking to move overseas during the 1970s. Though Charles, Greaves and Law had all played in Italy during the 1960s, few had followed them. From the late sixties, however, there was an alternative destination to Europe, without the language barrier – the North American Soccer League (NASL), active between 1968 and 1984. At the height of its mid-70s popularity, top international players flocked to its teams, including Pelé, Franz Beckenbauer, Johan Cruyff and Eusébio. With Welshman Phil Woosnam, a tireless advocate for the sport in the US, NASL commissioner from 1969 to 1983, and many British coaches, the biggest influx of players was from the Football League. A loan transfer to the NASL for the summer season was the most popular option; initially these tended to be

---

18 David Russell, *ibid.*

lesser-known players or those coming toward the end of their playing careers. Goalkeeper Kevin Keelan outlined its "obvious appeal to players like myself with years of League experience, who want a fresh challenge, and those up-and-coming youngsters who want to establish themselves in the League game."

As it became a lucrative proposition, more prominent figures arrived in the NASL, notably George Best and Rodney Marsh, plus 1966 World Cup winners Alan Ball, Gordon Banks, Geoff Hurst and Bobby Moore. The annual drain of players was significant, and of increasing concern when players in their prime, such as Trevor Francis, were loaned to American clubs with first call on their services. Frank Worthington, the First Division's top scorer in 1978/79, enjoyed loan spells at Philadelphia and Tampa Bay, declaring "It's a joy to play in the States. There is not so much pressure on you and the crowd appreciate you more." The mass exodus was not curbed until the Football League ended the practice of summer loans in 1979; after that, fewer British players chose to move permanently, and the NASL was itself coming to a close, though the various indoor leagues which had co-existed in the US were still an attractive option for some.

The League's main concern then, once more, became the potential spending power of major European clubs, sparked by the transfer of Kevin Keegan to Hamburg in 1977, where he became the German Bundesliga's highest-paid player, earning a reported £100,000 a year. Keegan's success – he was twice European Footballer of the Year, with Hamburg winning the Bundesliga in 1979, and reaching the European Cup Final the following year (where they lost to Nottingham Forest) – paved the way for others. In 1979, Laurie Cunningham became the first Englishman to sign for Real Madrid, where he played with distinction, while England striker Tony Woodcock joined another German club, Cologne. Cunningham summarised the attractions of a move abroad, stating that not only was he "keen to gain broader experience" but that, in England "the players are being poorly paid in comparison with other countries." These moves were the precursors to one of the significant trends of the 1980s, the transfers to European clubs of high-profile British players.

\*\*\*

Football hooliganism began to be regarded as a problem by the late 1960s, with the first Chester Report (1968) suggesting that "A club which allows its spectators to get out of hand may be heavily fined, as was Millwall in 1967, or have its ground closed for a period." This was soon followed by a 1969 report into crowd behaviour at matches, headed by John Lang, who concluded that "seating facilities could aid detection and apprehension of offenders". An FA enquiry into the death of a fan at a 1974 Blackpool match called for "seating all round the ground so that people can go to a match in safety". As violent incidents became more prevalent during the 1970s, Chelsea's response was to erect fences; in October 1972, eight-foot-high wire mesh was put up behind each goal at their Stamford Bridge ground to keep supporters off the pitch, which soon became commonplace.

The behaviour of Manchester United fans during their season in the Second Division (1974/75) led to Old Trafford having the first pitch-side perimeter fencing installed. By the later 1970s, clubs were looking to ban United's away following from their grounds while, after repeated trouble at their games, then-manager Tommy Docherty stated "I'm in favour of bringing back the birch." At different times, both Manchester United and Leeds United were banned from European competition, fined and suffered temporary ground closures as a result of serious crowd disturbances, as the authorities sought a solution to what was a social problem with serious implications for football.

The newly-established *Rothmans Football Yearbook* documented the game's major issues throughout the 1970s in a series of editorial articles; John Camkin opened the 1971/72 edition with a blunt statement: "Fewer goals are being scored than ever before. League attendances dropped by nearly 1.5m at a time when players' salaries and bonuses are rising at an alarming rate." He went on to detail "a depressing picture" of a game that was "dull and negative; rugged and hard; and resting for the most part, on insecure economic foundations." Sir Harold Thompson, on becoming FA Chairman in 1976, bemoaned the lack of entertainment, saying "The trouble is that our clubs cannot afford to lose matches", while adding "I understand their problem, but we must make an effort." At the very end of the decade, Jack Rollin's *Rothmans* editorial mirrored Camkin's concerns expressed at the start of it: "The game will never exist in any form if the gap between the clubs at the top and those in the bottom in any one division is allowed to grow."

The men who ran the clubs seemingly had few solutions to offer. Chairmen and Boards of Directors were often local businessmen and prominent townspeople, especially at provincial clubs. Many treated running a football club as an extension of their civic duty and saw their role as custodians rather than owners. Often derided for their lack of football knowledge, and rarely spending large amounts of their own money on the club, as a rule Chairmen were content to remain in the background. Only in a crisis, such as the dispute between Brian Clough and Sam Longson which led to Clough's departure from Derby County in 1973, would they receive publicity. Jimmy Hill at Coventry, rock star Elton John, who was prominent during Watford's rise to the First Division in the late 1970s-early 80s, and the outspoken Bob Lord of Burnley were among the exceptions.

Falling attendances and rising costs (not least for increased policing to combat hooliganism) left many clubs in a precarious financial position towards the end of the 1970s. However, those seeking success were still prepared to gamble by spending heavily on players, paying ever-increasing sums on both transfer fees and wages in a market which had become inflated since the abolition of the maximum wage and the Eastham verdict of the early 1960s, which ended the restrictions of the 'retain and transfer' system. The balance began to tip decisively toward the big-city clubs over the next two decades; once full freedom of contract was established in 1978, allowing players to negotiate with new employers at the end of their contract, both transfer fees and wages soon rose sharply.

Debt was rife throughout the League, with the additional costs of complying with the stadium regulations imposed by the 1975 Safety of Sports Grounds Act. No League club moved ground in the decade, preferring to renovate existing stadia, often commissioning new stands designed to generate commercial revenue and improve the spectator experience; Chelsea and Wolves were both close to liquidation as a result of hugely expensive re-building projects. The Football League at all levels headed into the 1980s caught in this vicious circle of spiralling costs and dwindling attendances, exacerbated by crowd violence inside and outside grounds. The game was in urgent need of new income, the main sources of which proved to be sponsorship and television.

# Sponsorship

Advertisements can be seen on pitch-side hoardings and grandstands in images of the League's earliest days – later the match-day programme became another vehicle for commercial revenue, often carrying promotions for local businesses, beer and cigarettes, products which individual players including Dixie Dean were happy to endorse. In the post-war era, leading players such as Stanley Matthews and Denis Compton (a dashing England international cricketer and Arsenal footballer who was known as 'the Brylcreem Boy') began to supplement their commercial income.

With the rise of players' agents, off-field activities became increasingly lucrative, especially in the sixties, where George Best was once again a pioneer with "the ghosted newspaper column, the modelling, the endorsements for hair tonic, chewing gum and Stylo Matchmakers football boots." Fuelled by England's 1966 World Cup win and media-friendly stars such as Best, the game began to see the potential returns of tapping into consumer culture.

In the seventies, with Best in decline, Kevin Keegan, Liverpool and England's clean-cut star, became the new marketable commodity, forming his own company, releasing a pop single *("It ain't easy")* and writing a newspaper column. Keegan, hard-working but less naturally gifted than Best, took a more cautious approach to celebrity, admitting "I set out to conduct myself differently from Bestie. I tried to learn from his mistakes." Keegan inherited Best's contract with Stylo, the boot-makers, and his name appeared on a range of products throughout the decade, including another pop single while he was playing in Germany, *"Head over heels in love."* This trend of branching out from football and establishing an identifiable 'brand' set the template for players to maximise their earnings in the decades to follow.

There was also a burgeoning industry for football merchandise, notably promotional material (commemorative coins, badges, figures) and sticker albums available to the public for the first time from newspapers and petrol stations. The Italian company Panini, founded in 1961, produced their first World Cup sticker album to coincide with the Mexico finals of 1970 and moved into the English market for the 1977/78 season. Throughout the League, clubs sought to increase off-field revenues, running lotteries, opening shops at the stadium and offering sponsorship opportunities for local firms around the ground, in the official programme, and even items of players' kit or the match ball. After retiring as a player, Jimmy Hill, instigator of the campaign to abolish the maximum wage, was appointed as manager of Coventry City in 1961. He immediately established himself as a marketing innovator, restoring the club strip to all-sky blue (and penning the *Sky Blue Song*), introducing an electronic scoreboard in 1964, the first colour match-day programme and, crucially, organising pre-match entertainment and community events at their Highfield Road ground.

The creeping commercialisation of the game was emphasised by the pioneering deal struck between Leeds United and kit manufacturer Admiral, at the instigation of manager Don Revie. In 1973/74, Leeds became the first top-flight English side to carry visible branding on their kit – the distinctive company logo appeared not only on team shirts but on the players' tracksuits (which also carried their names). It was part of a general marketing campaign which also saw the team kick branded footballs into the crowd before games, and the introduction of the iconic 'smiley' LUFC badge, all overseen by Revie, who had changed the Leeds colours from their traditional blue and gold to all-white in 1961, to emulate the great Real Madrid side of the time.

When he became manager of the national team at the end of the 1973/74 season, Revie ensured that the Admiral agreement was extended to England's kit, which carried a manufacturer's logo for the first time after the FA signed a five-year contract for a starting payment of £15,000 a year or a 10 per cent royalty. Though Bukta had manufactured kit for Nottingham Forest as early as the 1880s, and Umbro secured the very first exclusive contract for official England kit in 1952, these Admiral deals were the most significant steps toward today's multi-million-pound replica kit industry. As England manager, Revie remained an advocate for commercial income, publicly stating, "the quicker we realise sponsorship is the answer the better it will be for the game."[19]

Whilst advertisements for various companies around football grounds were long-established, the game's governing bodies continued to legislate against sponsorship on team shirts until the end of the 1970s. It was approved in the 1977/78 season but initially stymied by the refusal of television companies to broadcast fixtures featuring shirt sponsors. Non-league Kettering Town were in fact the first British team to have a sponsor's name on their shirts, in January 1976, though it was eventually removed after threats of fines from the FA. The club were then managed by Derek Dougan, former player and PFA Chairman, who argued that football's traditional reliance on gate income could no longer be sustained in the modern era. Dougan believed that allowing shirt sponsorship was "guaranteeing funds when the turnstiles cannot click enough to wipe out overdrafts and debts."[20]

With Kettering's attempt rejected, it was Scottish Premier League side Hibernian who became the first top-level British team to appear in sponsored shirts, advertising the Greater Manchester-based kit-maker Bukta, in 1977. They would have been joined by Derby County, who had a deal with Saab, and wore the shirts for a pre-season photo-shoot (the players also drove sponsored Saab cars) but the League had not yet given approval.

Liverpool became the first Football League club to have a sponsor's name on their shirts when they signed a two-year £100,000 contract with Japanese electronics firm Hitachi in 1979, with the stipulation that they would not be worn in European competition or televised domestic fixtures. By the start of the 1980/81 season, six First Division clubs had secured shirt sponsors. One of the most overt examples of sponsorship was Coventry City's partnership in the early 1980s with car

---

19 As reported in *The Times*, 20 August 1976
20 Derek Dougan, *How Not To Run Football*, 1981

manufacturers Talbot, whose logo dominated their shirt. It is believed that the ever-innovative Jimmy Hill, by now club Chairman, at one stage explored the possibility of renaming the club as 'Coventry Talbot,' which was flatly rejected.

Though traditionalists fumed and television held out briefly, with the BBC and ITV both refusing to show highlights of teams carrying sponsorship until 1983 (resulting on occasion in the sponsors' names being covered up for televised matches), the encroachment of advertising was impossible to turn back. Shirt sponsorship became the norm by the mid-1980s, ubiquitous across the four divisions of the Football League. The value of on-shirt advertising for both clubs and sponsoring companies only increased, as the benefits of wider exposure via television became apparent.

There had been sponsored cup competitions from the early 1970s, notably the Texaco and Watney Cups, both of which began in 1970. The latter had the distinction of becoming Britain's first-ever sponsored football competition, and settling drawn games by introducing penalty shoot-outs to the UK. They were followed by the experiment of the Ford Sporting League,[21] which lasted only during the 1970/71 season. It operated within league fixtures, by rewarding goals and discipline; teams were awarded a point for every goal scored at home and two for away goals, but had five points deducted for a booking and ten for sendings-off. Having turned down sponsorship offers in the 1970s, the first major domestic competition to take a sponsor's name was the League Cup. From 1982, it was funded by the Milk Marketing Board at £250,000 a year, hence becoming the Milk Cup until 1986; subsequent sponsors were clothing company Littlewoods, and Rumbelows, an electrical retailer.

The Football League itself accepted sponsorship from the Japanese company Canon in 1983 for £3.2 million over three years, at the time the most lucrative contract in British sport. That deal was followed by a season as the Today League, after a short-lived newspaper, until in 1987 Barclays Bank paid £4.5 million for naming rights. Each of these sponsorship agreements distributed money throughout the League's four divisions.

---

21 The Ford Sporting League was won by Oldham Athletic.

The FA Cup, which former Sports Minister Denis Howell had declared "The one event that I do not expect to see sponsored in my lifetime... it would hardly be British," resisted until 1994.[22] For the next four years, the competition was known as 'the FA Cup sponsored by Littlewoods.'

The notion of football itself as a marketable product, an identifiable brand, had been established by the 1980s. The long-serving Arsenal Chairman, Peter Hill-Wood, summed up the attitude of many within the game when he confessed "I was against advertising and sponsorship more than anyone. I felt we would be losing a little bit of our identity but I have been persuaded the other way." Alongside television deals, commercial ventures were increasingly seen as an essential revenue generator and drove the bigger clubs toward the idea of a breakaway from the rest of the League, in order to maximise those revenues for themselves.

---

22 Howell died in 1998.

# The Transfer Market (Part Two)

By the 1970s, fears of the inflation of the market, which had grown since the abolition of the maximum wage a decade earlier, were rife as fees spiralled and successive records were rapidly set, and broken, in turn – from Martin Peters' £200,000 move in March 1970 to Kevin Keegan's £500,000 transfer to Hamburg in June 1977. Despite recurrent concerns over excessive player values, in 1975 *The Sportsman's World of Soccer* was able to echo Sports Minister Denis Howell's sentiments and state that "at least the money stays in the game".

For the next couple of decades this held true, with the transfer market operating as a primitive form of wealth re-distribution through the divisions of the Football League. Many lower-division clubs remained solvent by selling their better players to buyers higher up in the league system. In several instances, players went from non-league straight to the First Division and, in the case of Alan Devonshire, Stuart Pearce, Cyrille Regis and Graham Roberts, into the England team. Throughout the 1980s, moves from the bottom to the top of the Football League continued to be a common occurrence, supplementing the finances of the lower divisions. With the emergence of the 'superstar' player and escalating fees, transfer revenue would increasingly be diverted into the accounts of agents, and later outside the English game altogether.

In February 1979, only a month after West Bromwich Albion paid £516,000 for David Mills, the seven-figure barrier was broken. Brian Clough took the bold step of making Trevor Francis Britain's first million-pound footballer when he signed him for Nottingham Forest from Birmingham City. Recognising the pressure this would put on the player, the transfer was set officially at £999,999.99, but associated fees took it over the historic £1 million mark. There were a dozen more million-pound-plus transfers in the next two years, while Second Division West Ham United paid a world record fee for a goalkeeper when spending £565,000 on Phil Parkes.

After the spate of million-pound transfers which followed Francis's landmark move, the Football League, fearing such spending could prove unsustainable given dwindling attendances and precarious finances, legislated to restrict this lavish outlay. At their June 1982 AGM, the League voted to amend transfer regulations, meaning that all fees had to be paid in full within 12 months of the transfer being completed, with at least half of the total to be paid when the transfer was first finalised. Clubs had previously paid gradually, in instalments stretching over several seasons and, in the straitened economic climate of the time, were unlikely to find the funds to pay up-front. This ensured that the £1.5 million which Manchester United paid West Brom for Bryan Robson in October 1981 remained the highest transfer fee between English clubs for six years, until Liverpool signed Peter Beardsley from Newcastle United for £1.9 million.

After the restriction on domestic transfer fees, a number of high-profile players subsequently went abroad; following Robson's 1981 transfer, the next seven record transfers involving English clubs were all sales to French, Italian or Spanish sides, a trend amplified by the ban from European competition imposed after the Heysel disaster of 1985. The moves which began with Keegan, Cunningham and Woodcock at the end of the 1970s, continued for over a decade, with Liam Brady, Luther Blissett, Steve Archibald, Trevor Francis, Mark Hateley, Ray Wilkins, Mark Hughes, Ian Rush, Gary Lineker, Glenn Hoddle and Chris Waddle amongst those leaving for European clubs, often for fees well in excess of £2 million.

Domestic transfer fees only began to rise once more towards the end of the 1980s, as the increased share of television money gave top-tier teams greater spending power; the first £2 million fee paid by an English club came in the summer of 1988, when Tottenham Hotspur signed Paul Gascoigne from Newcastle United. Within weeks of Gascoigne's transfer, the national record was broken again when Tony Cottee moved from West Ham United to Everton for £2.2 million, and once more, shortly afterwards, when Ian Rush returned to Liverpool from Juventus for £2.8 million. Those figures still lagged behind the sums routinely paid by Italian and Spanish clubs in particular; as late as 1992, a decade after the world's first £3 million transfer, the English record fee was set that year at £3.6 million, when Alan Shearer moved to Blackburn Rovers from Southampton.

It was not until the Premier League era that English clubs began to match, and then overtake, their Continental rivals for spending power. The early years of that competition saw rapidly escalating fees marked by Andy Cole's landmark move to Manchester United for £7 million in 1995, itself shortly eclipsed by Shearer's next transfer a year later, to Newcastle United; at £15 million this was not only a British, but a world, record fee, illustrating the shifting balance of financial dominance from Europe to the Premier League.

## Progress of British Transfer Record (1961-92)

|  |  |  |
|---|---|---|
| Jun 1961 | Gerry Hitchens (Aston Villa-Inter) | £85k |
| Jul 1962 | Denis Law (Torino-Manchester U) | £115k |
| Jun 1968 | Allan Clarke (Fulham-Leicester) | £150k |
| Jun 1969 | Allan Clarke (Leicester-Leeds) | £165k |
| Mar 1970 | Martin Peters (West Ham-Tottenham) | £200k |
| Dec 1971 | Alan Ball (Everton-Arsenal) | £220k |
| Aug 1972 | David Nish (Leicester-Derby) | £225k |
| Feb 1974 | Bob Latchford (Birmingham-Everton) | £350k |
| Jun 1977 | Kevin Keegan (Liverpool-Hamburg) | £500k |
| Jan 1979 | David Mills (Middlesbrough-West Brom) | £516k |
| Feb 1979 | Trevor Francis (Birmingham-N Forest) | £1m |
| Sep 1979 | Steve Daley (Wolves-Manchester C) | £1.45m |
| Sep 1979 | Andy Gray (Aston Villa-Wolves) | £1.469m |
| Oct 1981 | Bryan Robson (West Brom-Manchester U) | £1.5m |
| May 1986 | Mark Hughes (Manchester U-Barcelona) | £2.3m |
| Jun 1987 | Ian Rush (Liverpool-Juventus) | £3.2m |
| Jul 1989 | Chris Waddle (Tottenham-Marseille) | £4.25m |
| Jul 1991 | David Platt (Aston Villa-Bari) | £5.5m |

# The 1980s

"Professional football is a mirror of its time, reflecting society and sometimes, like theatre, exaggerating it; and in a period of chronic economic uncertainty, affluence but also unemployment, changing leisure patterns, protest and dissent, increasing violence and new technology the Football League was now faced by more problems than at any time in a hundred years." Bryon Butler, *The Official Illustrated History of the Football League*

The biggest shadows on football in the 1980s were precarious finances, increasing hooliganism and the associated issue of the dilapidated state of many stadiums. The gap between rich and poor in the Football League threatened to become a decisive split, with the top clubs demanding "fewer midweek fixtures, a 75 per cent share of television money for First Division clubs, separate sponsorship for the First Division and retention of gate receipts by the home clubs." Once again, Sir Norman Chester was asked to head a Committee of enquiry into the state of the national game, delivering a wide-ranging report in 1983, although many of his recommendations were ignored.

Much of this second Chester Report focussed on football's financial crisis, with about eighty of the ninety-two Football League clubs reckoned to be technically insolvent by the middle of the decade. The proposed solutions included once again a return to the regionalisation of the lower divisions, and a reduction in the size of the League (from 92 to 64 or 68 clubs), which were both rejected. At the same time, the top teams, faced with spiralling wages and dwindling attendances, were angling for a greater share of gate and television income. Chester was told by Everton Chairman Philip Carter that "the First Division clubs are becoming increasingly intolerant of a situation where they are required to subsidise clubs in the lower divisions". Carter was later quoted in *The Times* stating that "we must concentrate on the senior clubs."[23]

Chester suggested allowing home teams to keep the entirety of gate receipts, which had historically been shared with the away team. This recommendation was adopted, and increased the financial dominance of big-city clubs with larger attendances; a concession which satisfied them for the time being, but also sowed the seeds for an eventual breakaway from the Football League. As related in *Football Nation*:

> "The top clubs had requested a feasibility study for a Super (or Premier) League. Chester penned a private note: 'The top clubs know... that if they were free agents they would be likely to secure for themselves a much higher revenue than if they are treated as but part of ninety-two clubs. This is the issue which, if not settled amicably in the near future, could split the League.'"

In addition to continued violence by followers of the England team abroad, domestic football in the 1980s was plagued by hooliganism, and was searching for solutions before and after the Heysel Stadium disaster. At home, matters came to a head with the March 1985 pitch invasion by Millwall fans at Luton Town's Kenilworth Road, at a televised game. The government responded, with Prime Minister Margaret Thatcher, whose dislike of football was well known,[24] personally intervening. At a meeting with the Football Association and Football League on 1st April 1985, she recommended the installation of CCTV, a ban on alcohol at grounds, searching of fans, better segregation and more use of police intelligence. A six-point action plan was agreed, which incorporated Thatcher's recommendations, including membership schemes, more ticket-only matches and the 'installation of more effective perimeter fences around pitches.' As a result, Luton were "ordered by the FA to fence the entire perimeter of their ground".

---

23 *The Times*, 12 November 1985
24 Thatcher was described as "a bully who despised football" by former FA Chief Executive Graham Kelly

David Evans, Chairman of Luton Town and Conservative politician, had more radical plans, further instituting a ban on away fans and "a controversial membership-only scheme for fans under which only members were allowed to attend matches at the club's home ground." Later, in April 1985, after a pitch invasion at Stamford Bridge, Chelsea Chairman Ken Bates "installed a 12-foot high, barbed electric fence all around the pitch to pen in the fans and keep them in check." The Greater London Council, with responsibility for issuing safety certificates, intervened with the threat of legal action before the barrier's 12-volt charge could be turned on, believing it contravened the Safety of Sports Grounds Act 1975. It was dismantled shortly afterwards. Thatcher advocated compulsory ID cards for all football fans, a measure included in the 1989 Football Spectators Act, though never implemented in the face of a groundswell of political and public opposition.

The crises of neglected stadium infrastructure and worsening crowd behaviour culminated devastatingly in May 1985. On Saturday 11th May, a fire at Bradford City's Valley Parade stadium claimed the lives of 56 supporters, spreading rapidly through the antiquated wooden main stand. The structure had been built in 1908 and, known to be 'an unacceptable fire hazard' due to the decades of accumulated litter beneath it, was due for demolition two days after the game. On the same day, violent clashes at Birmingham City's St Andrews ground, where Leeds United were the visitors, resulted in the death of a young fan. Chief Constable of West Midlands Police, Geoffrey Dear, described the scenes as "possibly the worst crowd disorders ever seen at a football ground in this country" in his annual report.

Only weeks later, on Wednesday 29th May 1985, another tragedy occurred before the European Cup Final staged at Brussels' Heysel Stadium. Violence, judged by investigators to have been instigated by Liverpool fans, resulted in the deaths of another 39 supporters, most of them Italian, when a wall collapsed. Criminal prosecutions followed, as 26 Liverpool fans were charged with manslaughter, while the poor state of the stadium also came under scrutiny; both clubs had requested a change of venue, believing Heysel was not in any condition to host a European Final. UEFA, as the governing body, refused this request.

The proximity of the disasters of Birmingham, Bradford and Heysel meant that, taken together, they represented the lowest point in the history of English professional football. In several instances, they were deliberately conflated, despite their different causes. *The Sunday Times* responded to the Bradford fire in an editorial entitled 'Putting the boot in,' connecting "football hooligans [who have] brought thuggery and blood to the terraces ... throughout the season" to "the worst blow of all – the appalling and inexcusable death-by-fire of 52 [later 56] fans".[25] In the wake of Heysel, the same paper was prompted to label the game "a slum sport, played in slum stadiums, increasingly watched by slum people".[26] English clubs were promptly barred from European competition by UEFA for "an indeterminate period of time". The ban, which lasted for five years, was not extended to the national team, despite its followers causing repeated trouble abroad.

In retrospect, separating Bradford and Heysel shows how each tragically highlighted major failings within English football, which the subsequent enquiries only partially addressed. Sadly, it took yet another tragedy to provide the impetus for lasting change.

It was the Hillsborough stadium disaster of April 1989, when 96 Liverpool fans died in the overcrowded Leppings Lane end at an FA Cup semi-final, which finally proved the catalyst for far-reaching changes in the English game. There had been serious crushes at the same end of the stadium during the 1981 and 1987 semi-finals, but these warnings went unheeded. In the aftermath of the 1989 tragedy, Lord Justice Taylor concluded that "although there were other causes, the main reason for the disaster was the failure of police control." His report made 76 recommendations, concentrating on stadium design, including the crush barriers, fencing and turnstiles which had all played a part in the disaster, but also covered the sale of alcohol within grounds, and ticket prices. Many of his suggestions were not implemented, but the Taylor Report had the primary effect of leading to a government directive that standing was unsafe at top-level football matches.

---

25 *Sunday Times* editorial, 19 May 1985
26 *Sunday Times* editorial, 2 June 1985

The initial ruling that the Hillsborough deaths were accidental was subsequently challenged, though it took until 2016 for an enquiry to reach a verdict of unlawful killing; jurors found the-then match commander, South Yorkshire Police Chief Superintendent David Duckenfield, "responsible for manslaughter by gross negligence" due to breaching his duty of care toward spectators. Despite a concerted effort by the police and several media outlets to blame the fans for the disaster, a combination of inadequate safety provisions at the ground, perimeter fences, terraced 'pens' and the policing of the game, initially highlighted in the Taylor Report, was largely responsible. Hillsborough was a legacy of decades of under-investment in infrastructure and attitudes toward football fans, which had hardened into policies which prioritised containment and confrontation over safety.

***

After the Bradford fire, the dangerously dilapidated state of many grounds, particularly in the lower divisions, was finally addressed in an official inquiry, chaired by Sir Oliver Popplewell. His report unfortunately included the events at Birmingham together with those at Bradford – according to Anthony King, a confusion which emphasised "the repressive control of the crowd above the architectural safety of the ground."[27] Popplewell ruled out all-seater stadia (on the basis that hooligans might use seats as weapons) but recommended "the introduction of close-circuit television at League grounds" and "endorsed the presence of perimeter fences as a means of control." Whilst partially discredited by Hillsborough, the Popplewell Inquiry gave an initial push toward new stadia which was to become a theme over following decades.

Though few clubs had the finances to implement the wholesale changes required to render them completely safe, Scunthorpe United opted for a radical solution in moving to a purpose-built ground. Their new home, Glanford Park, opened in 1988, was the first League stadium to be built in England for 33 years, since Southend United had moved to Roots Hall in 1955.

27 Anthony King, *The Premier League and the New Consumption of Football* (1995)

This move set the template for future re-locations; Scunthorpe were unable to afford the necessary improvements to their stadium – The Old Showground, built circa 1867 – in the wake of recommendations made by the Popplewell Inquiry. The only viable option was for them to move from their long-established, town-centre location to a purpose-built, out-of-town site. 23 League clubs followed suit between 1988 and 2007, typically funding the move by selling their old ground to a supermarket chain or housing developer.

This trend was given impetus by the Taylor Report, commissioned after the 1989 Hillsborough disaster, which "stipulated that all Football League grounds should be all-seaters for safety reasons" (a proposal later limited to the top two English divisions and the Scottish Premier League). All-seater stadia represented a considerable investment for smaller clubs, who remained heavily dependent on match-day income and lacked the commercial power of the top teams. In many instances, moving to another site was a cheaper option than redeveloping ageing stadia; other clubs saw it as an opportunity to increase their ground capacity and maximise revenues. Prices rose sharply, initially to pay for the move or installation of seating and general stadium re-development, latterly to help cover the soaring costs of players' wages, with a knock-on effect on attendances in the lower divisions.

After the long-standing rules guaranteeing 20% of gate receipts for the away side were changed in 1983, a crucial source of revenue from which smaller teams had traditionally benefitted when visiting bigger clubs was removed. The levy of 4% which was taken from all gate receipts and redistributed evenly between the 92 League clubs at the end of each season was reduced to 3% in 1985 (when the First Division also secured a larger share of television money). It was clear that the richer teams were intent on removing these forms of 'subsidy' to the rest, and retaining any profit to be made for themselves – the gate receipt levy finally ceased completely with the arrival of the Premier League. Only the FA Cup retained the historic, egalitarian gate-sharing principle of the League's formation, and to be drawn against a top club in the Cup remains a valuable pay-day for the lower leagues.

Ken Bates was among a new breed of entrepreneurial football club owner, having previously been Chairman at Oldham

Athletic in the 1960s, and on the board of Wigan Athletic from 1980 until he purchased debt-ridden Chelsea for £1 in 1982. The London club was founded by Gus Mears and had been run ever since by his descendants; clubs were often handed down as a family business – Arsenal had three generations of Hill-Woods as Chairmen, while the Cobbold family had a similar dynasty at Ipswich Town. This model of paternalistic ownership began to fracture in the 1980s – newspaper mogul Robert Maxwell bought Oxford United in the same year as Bates' purchase of Chelsea, before taking a share in Derby County later in the decade, though he was thwarted in his attempt at a take-over of Manchester United.

Maxwell attempted to merge Oxford and Reading into the 'Thames Valley Royals' in 1983, arguing the clubs were not economically viable as separate entities. Though that move was rejected, the idea was revived four years later by QPR Chairman David Bulstrode. He proposed merging with neighbours Fulham, selling their historic Craven Cottage ground and continuing as 'Fulham Park Rangers.' Bulstrode stated that Fulham's fans "will appreciate it is not economical in the long run for the club to continue on its own". While mergers were strongly opposed, other radical solutions to football's financial problems were undertaken. After taking control of Tottenham Hotspur in 1982, property developer Irving Scholar oversaw their flotation on the Stock Exchange, a first for any sports club in the world, and was instrumental in the push for a larger share of television revenue for the major clubs. At this stage, there was no suggestion of overseas investment in English football.

***

On the field, in the last full decade of the Football League, it was still possible for provincial clubs to compete, and thrive, as evidenced by Ipswich Town, Southampton, and Watford, who were all First Division runners-up between 1980 and 1984. The opportunity for clubs to move through the leagues remained; most spectacularly in the cases of Swansea City and Wimbledon, both of whom followed Watford from the bottom to the top division for the first time in the course of a few short years. Swansea illustrated the unpredictability of the League system by promptly dropping back to the lowest tier by 1986, having finished the 1981/82 season in sixth place in the First Division. Founder members of the Football League in 1888, Burnley and Wolverhampton Wanderers, both post-war Champions, fell on hard times and dropped into the Fourth Division for the first time in their long and distinguished histories.

Yet there were growing problems on and off the pitch, and a widespread recognition that change was needed. To increase the competitiveness of the League, automatic promotion and relegation to and from the League was introduced in the 1986/87 season. This finally ended the arbitrary and often unfair practice of clubs applying for re-election, which had effectively created a closed shop. In the same year, there was further reform in the creation of the play-off system, which ensured that more clubs retained an interest in potential promotion until the very end of the season, instead of the top places being assured weeks in advance. Typical of a generally positive reception, Stuart Jones of *The Times* wrote that "The welcome change in the antiquated system will clearly introduce added tension and excitement at the season's end." Initially, teams from the higher division competed in the play-offs against those challenging for promotion, which allowed Charlton Athletic to retain their First Division status in May 1987. By the start of the following season, the League allowed clubs to name and use a second substitute for the first time since their introduction in 1965. From then, the number of substitutes only increased again with the inception of the Premier League.

The seeds of future inequality between clubs even within the top division, sown over previous decades, were becoming increasingly apparent. At the start of the 1980s, even as he was guiding Aston Villa to a first League title for 71 years, manager Ron Saunders foresaw a day when the top teams would form an elite competition: "Sooner or later, there are going to be only a handful of clubs who can compete at the current level, and they will form a Super League." The ensuing arguments during the decade over the allocation of income from television (covered in detail by a later section), driven by the richest clubs, further indicated that English football would move in the direction of Saunders' prediction in the near future.

The years preceding the Premier League were the last era of the FA Cup as a major trophy, with every club fielding a full-strength team, semi-finals played at various neutral grounds around the country, and the Wembley final the season's showpiece, an international spectacle. The tournament was still regarded as the world's most prestigious club competition, containing all the excitement and unpredictability of cup football, with West Ham United, Coventry City and Wimbledon all among the seven different winners during the decade. This continued evidence of the FA Cup's democratic tradition followed unlikely triumphs for Sunderland, Southampton and Ipswich Town in the 1970s, when nine different clubs won the trophy. In contrast, to date the same total of nine teams have lifted the FA Cup since 1993, with only Portsmouth and Wigan Athletic regarded as genuine surprise winners.

There were still the famous 'giant-killings' from 1980 to 1992, where lower-level teams managed to defeat teams from the top division. These ranged from Halifax Town's victory over Manchester City in 1980, through non-league Sutton United's triumph over Coventry City in 1989, to Wrexham knocking out reigning League champions Arsenal in 1992. The League Cup too remained a major domestic honour, won by smaller clubs such as Norwich City, Oxford United, and Luton Town; Oldham Athletic reached the final as late as 1990.

A Jimmy Hill-led initiative intended to boost crowd numbers was the introduction of three points for a win in 1981, after nearly one hundred years of two points being awarded for a League victory. There was growing criticism of defensive football – coaches and managers had to be pragmatic in a results-driven business, an attitude summarised by Stoke manager Alan Durban in 1980: "if you want entertainment, you could go out and get a bunch of clowns." Hill and, eventually, the Football League, felt the climate of negative play and safety-first tactics was a factor in alienating the fans. The change to three points was designed to provide an incentive for attacking football, as it was believed that it would encourage teams to play for a win rather than settle for the single point of a drawn game.

Though goals-per-game in the top division actually fell in the first season of three points for a win, it began to rise in the mid-1980s. Goal-scoring levels have in fact remained fairly static since the early 1970s through the Premier League era, with the 1967/68 First Division the last top-flight season to record an average of over three goals per game. While the effect of the extra point on attendances was not immediately apparent, the idea was rapidly accepted and adopted across the world, finally being used for the group stages of the World Cup Finals of 1994.

English football continued to wrestle with methods of improving entertainment and thus attendances at grounds. An emphasis on defending, the popularity of the 'long ball,' time-wasting and the excessive use of the back-pass all caused concern. The back-pass in particular, to a goalkeeper who would pick the ball up at leisure and hang on to it for as long as possible, was designed to stifle the flow of a game, especially for sides protecting a lead. Despite periodic instructions for referees to clamp down on foul play, the tough treatment which had been meted out to George Best and other 'flair' players over the years was by and large accepted as part and parcel of the game. Playing conditions lent themselves to a physical game, with fierce tackling a traditional characteristic of English football.

Another innovation designed to improve the game as a spectacle was the use of artificial pitches, which promised a perfect playing surface all year round. Especially in mid-winter, Football League fixtures were often played in conditions resembling a mud-bath; one of the most notoriously boggy pitches was at Derby County's Baseball Ground. The idea had been mooted as early as the 1960s by Eric Taylor, General Manager of Sheffield Wednesday, who had been impressed by a visit to the Houston Astrodome, seeking a general improvement in playing facilities. In Houston, he had been introduced to Astroturf, a blend of synthetic fibres resembling natural grass, invented specifically for indoor sport. Taylor commented enthusiastically: "that turf is marvellous. It has the advantage, too, of never altering. It means that people who have spent three or four pounds on a ticket are not going to have the spectacle spoiled because the pitch is wet or muddy. It would mean a consistent surface with the consequent result of consistently good football from the good players."

Despite this endorsement, and the apparently deteriorating state of pitches at many League grounds, the cheaper alternative was not adopted until 1981, when QPR became the first side to introduce an artificial playing surface, known as 'Omniturf.'

They were later followed by Luton Town, Oldham Athletic and Preston North End, but the early synthetic surfaces were criticised by grass traditionalists for their abnormal bounce and the potential for damage to players' limbs. The FA outlawed these 'plastic pitches' in 1995, though they continue to be used for professional football in other parts of the world, with advances in technology allowing them to replicate real turf much more closely than the 1980s prototypes.

Overall, Everton and especially Liverpool were the dominant clubs in domestic competition, winning eight League titles between them, challenged by Arsenal towards the end of the decade. The era of Liverpool's success, continuing from the 1970s, saw Championship trophies distributed around the north and midlands, but was a barren period for London and the south. When Arsenal finally became Champions with a dramatic win at Anfield in 1989, it was the first title for a London club in 18 years, since their 'double' of 1971. English teams continued to excel in Europe, with wins for Nottingham Forest, Liverpool and Aston Villa in the European Cup, Everton in the Cup Winners' Cup, and Ipswich Town and Tottenham Hotspur in the UEFA Cup. This success came to an abrupt end with the ban imposed in the wake of the Heysel disaster; English clubs were only re-admitted to European competition five years later, in 1990. The final season of the unified Football League, 1991/92, saw Leeds United win their first Championship since the 1970s; their manager, Howard Wilkinson, remains (to date) the last Englishman to win the title.

\*\*\*

A major factor in football's rehabilitation was the improvement of the national team under Bobby Robson, Ipswich Town's successful manager of the 1970s and early 80s. After struggling initially when England failed to qualify for the 1984 European Championships, Robson took England to a creditable quarter-final at the 1986 World Cup in Mexico, and defeat at the hand of Diego Maradona. After a disastrous campaign at the 1988 European Championships, losing all three group games, Robson's side peaked at the World Cup of Italia '90. Reaching the semi-finals, where they lost on penalties to old adversaries West Germany, represented England's best performance since 1966 and sparked a similar boom in interest. The renaissance of the national side was symbolised by the celebrity of the team's new star, Paul Gascoigne, and his tears after he received the booking which would have ruled him out of the final. The spectacle of the finals indicated a future for football watched in modern stadia and broadcast worldwide to a paying audience.

Football, an unfashionable interest for all but the dwindling number attending games in the 1980s, gradually became popular once more; supporters found their voice accepted, as the burgeoning fanzine culture gave rise to publications such as *When Saturday Comes, Total Football* and *FourFourTwo*. Media attitudes softened, and the hostility of the Thatcher government gave way to a realisation that there was not only money but political capital to be made out of the game, with both John Major and David Mellor happy to be identified as Chelsea fans. Despite the traditional indifference of the literary world, the game made it into the pages of *Granta* and *The London Review of Books*, as a number of authors portrayed the sport in a sympathetic light, notably Nick Hornby in his influential 1992 memoir, *Fever Pitch*.

There were many factors which contributed to the conditions for creating the Premier League, but it was ultimately the triple tragedies of Bradford, Heysel and Hillsborough that changed the shape of the game and how it was watched; a tragic illustration of David Goldblatt's observation that "The Edwardian infrastructure of the game was in visible decline."[28] The changes set in motion by Hillsborough and the subsequent Taylor Report, together with the boost of Italia '90, transformed the experience for spectators; perimeter fences were removed, together with terraces at most grounds. Aided by the improved stadium facilities and lucrative television deals, the top clubs actively marketed themselves to new consumers, seeking a bigger and more affluent audience.

---

28 Writing in *The Game of Our Lives: the Meaning and Making of English Football* (2014)

# Attendances

"The 1948/1949 season constituted the high-water mark in attendances at Football League games – there were 41.3 million match attendances that season – but from then until 1986, excepting a slight bulge after 1966, when England won the World Cup, attendances fell steadily."
Anthony King, *The End of the Terraces*

Falling attendances had been a persistent concern over the several decades in which they steadily declined from their post-war peak – largely blamed on a combination of economic climate, hooliganism, and lack of entertainment. During the following decades, crowds continued to fall – according to Bryon Butler in *The Official Illustrated History of the Football League*, "this was not surprising. The post-war boom belonged to a period of austerity and escape while attendances in the 'seventies reflected a different kind of society." The game's traditional working-class base had both more disposable income and increased leisure options.

Matt Busby was of the opinion that societal changes were the main factor behind this pattern, a view shared by *The Football League Review* in 1971, which stated, "The cause of declining attendances can be seen to be influenced by external leisure activities." A visit to a football ground was but one among many competing attractions on a Saturday afternoon, and the sport had to search for solutions to try and reverse the long-term trend of falling crowds. The League began to consider different options to attract more spectators – matches under floodlights had been introduced from 1956, a move given impetus by the introduction of the Football League Cup four years later, a competition specifically designed to take advantage of floodlit mid-week games. An experiment with Sunday football was seriously considered for the first time, after a 1967 National Opinion Poll found 75% of interviewees in favour of professional sport on Sundays. It took until 1974 for the League to stage fixtures on a Sunday, but it proved a short-lived experiment, soon abandoned after only a brief initial upswing in attendances.

There was general agreement that football's entertainment value had declined, and much energy was devoted to ideas for improving its appeal to spectators. The boom in popularity of the NASL in the 1970s was in part down to innovations such as awarding extra points for goals scored and deciding drawn games with penalty shoot-outs. However, the American league was appealing to a new audience, effectively starting from scratch, and not contending with the game's evolution over the best part of a century.

English venues themselves required attention though the clubs, facing rising wage bills and transfer fees, were reluctant to invest in their stadia. Nor were they prepared to lower admission prices, as gate income was, at that point, by far their main source of revenue. The state of Football League grounds by the early 1980s was captured in Simon Inglis's pioneering book *Football Grounds of England & Wales*. His study found a majority of clubs playing at venues that were still recognisable from their Victorian origins, many of which had fallen into terminal disrepair, and were to be abandoned completely in the near future. Both safety and spectator comfort had suffered from decades of neglect and, as the English game reached its lowest ebb in the wake of the 1985 Bradford fire, few would have predicted that football was to be completely transformed in the years ahead.

There had been sporadic efforts to improve facilities at grounds; Scottish club Clydebank created Britain's first all-seater stadium at Kilbowie Park in 1977, and Aberdeen soon followed, converting their Pittodrie ground between 1978 and 1980, at a cost of approximately £3 million. In the Football League, Jimmy Hill once more led the way, promoting such all-seater stadia as the solution to crowd trouble, stating "it's harder to be a hooligan when you're sitting down". Hill oversaw the conversion of Coventry City's Highfield Road ground to all-seating in 1981, despite suggestions that the revenue from higher ticket prices was an equally strong factor as deterring violence. Coventry's attendances actually fell by 6,000 over the following two seasons, as a substantial number of fans were disenchanted, complaining about the increased admission fees and loss of atmosphere within the stadium; terracing was restored by popular demand in 1983. Across the League, the preferred method of preventing hooliganism was pitch-side fencing to contain potential trouble-makers.

It was hoped that the combined measures of providing better facilities and combatting hooliganism would bring back the missing fans, but overall attendances continued to fall through the 1980s, dropping to less than half of the numbers reached in the halcyon post-war years. Ground improvements and crowd control respectively came too late to prevent the tragedies of May 1985 at Bradford City and the Heysel Stadium. The following season saw the aggregate Football League attendance fall to an all-time low of less than 16 and a half million. It was only from 1986/87 that attendances began to climb once more, and increased for each of the six remaining seasons prior to the formation of the Premier League, the first time this had happened since the Second World War.

## Attendance Records

### Football League – Highest

| | | | |
|---|---|---|---|
| **Div 1** | Manchester United v Arsenal | 83,260 | 17/01/1948 |
| | Chelsea v Arsenal | 82,905 | 12/10/1935 |
| | Manchester City v Arsenal | 79,491 | 23/02/1935 |
| | Everton v Liverpool | 78,299 | 18/09/1948 |
| | Chelsea v Blackpool | 77,696 | 16/10/1948 |
| | Everton v Preston North End | 76,839 | 28/08/1954 |
| | Chelsea v Arsenal | 75,952 | 09/10/1937 |
| | Everton v Wolves | 75,322 | 27/12/1954 |
| | Chelsea v Wolves | 75,043 | 09/04/1954 |
| | Manchester City v Arsenal | 74,918 | 10/04/1937 |

### Football League – Lowest

| | | | |
|---|---|---|---|
| **Div 3 (S)** | Thames v Luton Town | 469 | 06/12/1930 |
| **Div 3 (N)** | Gateshead v Doncaster R | 552 | 28/04/1934 |
| **Div 3** | Rochdale v Cambridge U | 588 | 05/02/1974 |
| **Div 3** | Gateshead v Accrington S | 622 | 26/03/1952 |
| **Div 4** | Scarborough v Wrexham | 625 | 07/12/1990 |
| **Div 3 (N)** | Ashington v Walsall | 630 | 04/04/1927 |
| **Div 3** | Chester City v Reading | 631 | 05/03/1991 |
| **Div 3 (N)** | Durham City v Wrexham | 641 | 28/04/1926 |
| **Div 3 (N)** | Wigan Borough v Barrow | 644 | 12/12/1926 |
| **Div 3 (N)** | Darlington v Tranmere R | 680 | 25/02/1933 |

Highest Post-War Season Aggregate Totals

| | |
|---|---|
| 1948/49 | 41,271,414 |
| 1949/50 | 40,517,865 |
| 1947/48 | 40,259,130 |
| 1950/51 | 39,584,967 |
| 1951/52 | 39,015,866 |

Lowest Post-War Season Aggregate Totals

| | |
|---|---|
| 1985/86 | 16,488,577 |
| 1986/87 | 17,379,218 |
| 1984/85 | 17,849,835 |
| 1987/88 | 17,959,732 |
| 1983/84 | 18,358,631 |

# Television

"While television is a contributory factor to falling gates, it would be wrong to put most of the blame in this direction. Handled the right way, TV can do the game a lot of good." Commentator John Motson, *Shoot!* Magazine, 1980

The debate about televised football, which had continued from the 1960s to the mid-80s, had effectively been settled by the time the Premier League came into being. The question of whether television is good for the game, and how much (if any) football should be televised, seems laughable today. However, it was the decisions made back in the eighties, in an era of dwindling attendances, that shaped the future of English football. At the time, few people could have looked beyond the short-term income, and anticipated the full scale of television's involvement. With the escalating Sky deals and sales of overseas broadcasting rights, the Premier League has enjoyed unprecedented wealth. Misgivings as to television's influence – on the fixture list and, with the introduction of VAR, events on the pitch – still surface occasionally. Yet the distribution of its revenue, once the Football League's central concern, is barely discussed; the big clubs won the argument, and there was no turning back.

\*\*\*

Whilst attendances had begun in any case to fall from their post-war peak, television was one of the key factors which accelerated their decline once football became available in the home. Television's dominance was a slow process; the only live games of the 1950s and early 60s were the FA Cup Final and sporadic international and World Cup fixtures. Both clubs and the game's authorities – the Football League in particular – were wary of the impact on attendances at grounds. From its inception in 1955, the new commercial broadcaster, Independent Television (ITV), had seen the potential market for televised football. The company had shown high-profile friendly matches, European and FA Cup ties, and were keen to add League games to their programming. To that end, ITV paid the Football League £150,000 for the rights to show live matches from the start of the 1960/61 season, after reaching agreement that coverage would only start at 7:30pm, at the end of the first half as kick-offs were set at 6:50. This payment was retained by the League and not shared among the clubs, prompting several of them to refuse to take part in televised games.

The very first attempt at screening a League game live, in September 1960, was such a failure that it would not be until 1983 that they became a regular feature. ITV had selected Blackpool v Bolton, gambling on the presence of Stanley Matthews, then 45 but still English football's biggest star. Unfortunately, he was injured; worse, the camera position chosen was behind one of the goals, severely restricting the view on the small screen and resulting in the commentator, Peter Lloyd, struggling to identify players throughout. After Bolton's dour single-goal victory, the deal was abandoned. When live League football finally returned, the television companies had all the benefits of advances in live-outside broadcast technology, such as improved definition, the action replay and slow-motion, which had simply not been available in the early 1960s.

The viewing public had to be content with highlights of selected matches on regional stations in the years before the BBC's *Match of the Day* programme on Saturday nights brought national coverage, in August 1964. The agreement provided for lower-league games to be featured alongside top-flight football. In 1968, with the arrival of colour television, ITV's *The Big Match* began broadcasting a Sunday afternoon highlights programme on London Weekend Television, with regional equivalents. Both networks supplemented their coverage by introducing studio discussions with panels of experts, including players and managers such as Malcolm Allison, Brian Clough, Derek Dougan and Jimmy Hill, one of the instigators of the concept.

Football League Secretary Hardaker remained sceptical of television's growing influence, observing that "too many sports have been ruined by allowing TV to run them. That won't happen to football." Burnley Chairman Bob Lord was also among the most outspoken critics of televised football, believing it would "damage and undermine attendances". The objections of Lord and others led to the long-standing arrangement that games would not be shown live at 3:00pm on Saturday.

Evidence that supported concerns about the effect of televised football on attendances accumulated; a National Opinion Poll Survey of December 1966 found that "38 per cent of all those who said they were interested in football did not attend because they could see matches on TV." The first Chester Report commented on the reasons given for refusing an offer (this time from the BBC) made in the late 1960s: "The League clubs fear that a regular weekly programme of live matches, selected by the BBC for their entertainment value, would be bound to reduce the incentive to attend the local ground".

While it was initially regarded cautiously by many within the game, it soon became clear that televised fixtures offered a reliable source of additional income, which was particularly welcome for struggling lower-division clubs. For these first highlights deals with television companies, the whole League benefitted financially – as a 2011 meeting of the Parliamentary Culture, Media & Sport Committee noted, "the same redistributive principle [as gate receipts] applied with the new revenue shared equally among all the League clubs." This arrangement remained in place throughout the 1960s and 70s. The combined total paid by the BBC and ITV for highlights packages was estimated to be in excess of £300,000 per season by the early seventies, with *Match of the Day* attracting audiences of 12 million.

Televised football proliferated through the 1970s and into the next decade, with the long-standing highlights programmes supplemented by the screening of full live games from 1983. The agreement was reached after lengthy negotiations when television companies compromised to allow on-screen shirt sponsorship. The contract, worth £5.2 million over two seasons, stipulated ten First Division matches to be shown live, five for each of the BBC and ITV (on Friday nights and Sunday afternoons respectively), with no club appearing more than once on each channel during the season. While it generated significant income – each of the 92 League clubs received £25,000, with additional payments to the featured teams – the old fears as to television's impact on attendances and disruption of the traditional fixture list were apparent, and much-discussed.

As a 'television man,' one of a number of ex-players and managers now employed as a commentator and pundit, Bob Wilson remained cautious about its influence, recognising the "danger of football becoming a slave to the sponsors and to TV". Fellow commentator John Motson was equally concerned about the game's potential dependence on television, conceding that "there is too much soccer on TV... the whole thing's mushroomed." The Fulham Chairman Ernie Clay was more forthright about the effects: "The cameras are wrecking our game because of over-exposure."

By the mid-80s it was clear that there was no resisting the tide of televised football; instead, the distribution of funds became the major issue. The bigger clubs had been agitating for a greater slice from the television deals for some time, and believed football was under-selling itself. The television companies themselves naturally favoured featuring those clubs who attracted the largest audiences, and future negotiations focussed on meeting their mutual interests.

In 1985, a dispute between the League and television led to a temporary TV blackout, to the consternation of the clubs known at the time as English football's 'Big Five' – Arsenal, Everton, Liverpool, Manchester United and Tottenham. Complaining that the League could no longer sustain a division of income among 92 clubs, the Big Five threatened a breakaway in order to secure a 50% share of television funds for the First Division. This did not satisfy them however, and their reliance on this source of income drove them to make still greater demands.

British Satellite Broadcasting entered the bidding when the next television contract was up for renewal in 1988, making an ambitious offer which was rejected in favour of a separate £44 million four-season deal negotiated with Greg Dyke of ITV. That agreement, entailing eighteen live games per season, allocated 75% to the top division in addition to bonuses for each featured match. From there the splitting of the League over television revenue became almost inevitable – as Ward & Williams recount in *Football Nation:*

In 1990, the Big Five had a discussion with Greg Dyke, now with London Weekend Television, about a breakaway of the First Division clubs – which would be financed by a new television contract, due for re-negotiation in 1992. Dyke told the club chairmen that he would be interested in covering such a breakaway 'Premier League.' Football was, after all, "the key television product in England."

In the event, the BBC-ITV duopoly was broken as the bidding war prompted by Dyke was won by BskyB, newly created by the merger of British Satellite Broadcasting with Sky. The satellite company, operating as Sky Sports and owned by Rupert Murdoch, paid £191 million for television rights to 60 games per year between 1992 and 1997. The entire First Division resigned from the Football League to form the new FA Premier League in May 1992, to take advantage of the riches on offer from the Sky television deal. Live football was no longer available for free to a domestic audience, who had to sign up for a subscription package in order to view games. Now competing for lucrative overseas rights, televised English league football was to be aggressively marketed to a global audience. Sky advertised their acquisition of exclusive live Premier League coverage as "a whole new ball game", and indeed it heralded a break from a 104-year history and the beginning of a new era for English football.

# Conclusion

"The reason for the formation of the Premier League was to re-brand football, make the game more commercially viable and to generate more money for the top clubs."
Matthew Bazell, *Theatre of Silence*

The last thirty years of the unified Football League saw a rapid growth in commercialisation, marked by the generation of significant income from sponsorship and televised league football. These new sources of revenue were needed to off-set the spiralling costs of transfer fees and players' contracts, which were set in motion by the abolition of the maximum wage in 1961. The hooliganism and racism prevalent at many football grounds in the 1970s and 80s made attending games an uncomfortable and, at times, dangerous experience. The neglect of spectator safety and violence surrounding the game culminated in the 1985 tragedies of Bradford and Heysel, one immediate consequence of which was an end to the dominance of English clubs in European competition. The unsustainable way the game was watched, and policed, was tragically reinforced by the Hillsborough disaster in 1989 and finally addressed by the Taylor Report, ushering in the era of all-seater stadia and leading many clubs to leave their traditional homes. A successful World Cup for the national team in 1990, steadily rising domestic attendances and sympathetic media coverage all contributed toward repairing the violent image of English football.

These were the conditions at the time the clubs of the top division voted to 'break away' from the Football League in 1992 and create a separate competition to maximise their revenue, in the form of the Premier League. While it was predictably hailed as "the biggest advance in TV football since the invention of the camera" by Dave Hill, head of sport at Sky TV, the successful bidder for television rights, respected figures within the game had misgivings. Steve Coppell, manager of Crystal Palace, was among the critics, believing "the big clubs will get richer". A similar sentiment was expressed by the man who would go on to become the Premier League's most successful manager; Alex Ferguson described its formation as "the most ludicrous and backward step football has taken for a long time."

\*\*\*

Inter-linked processes of commercialisation, gentrification and globalisation have changed the face of English football over the course of three decades, resulting in a decisive shift away from its working-class roots. The experience of attending a top-level football match has altered fundamentally during that period, transformed by rising prices and all-seater stadia. Many older fans bemoan the loss of atmosphere and the noise generated from vast terraces, together with the demolition of historic stands and whole grounds. The power of television, football's main benefactor, now dictates not only fixture dates and times (making the traditional Saturday three o'clock kick-off a rarity in the top flight), but decides the outcome of games via VAR.

The expansion of the Champions League in Europe has led to a scramble for places at the top of the Premier League and made a fourth-place finish more important than success in the domestic cup competitions. First-team players are routinely 'rested' from cup ties until the final, with clubs openly treating the FA Cup, once such a keenly-contested and sought-after prize, as an inconvenience. Squads and support staff, incorporating analysts and sports scientists, have grown hugely while training facilities have been overhauled and re-located together with stadia.

Football's adoption of the language of marketing gives a strong clue to the direction it has taken since 1992, where global branding and new revenue streams dictate the matchday experience and the product on the pitch. Players are commodities, traded for huge sums and generating millions in image rights. Sales of replica kit and merchandise, especially overseas, together with lucrative TV deals, means clubs no longer have to cultivate local support, and are increasingly removed from their roots; at the top level, income from attendances is dwarfed by off-field revenue. The priorities of modern football are further illustrated by the prominence of agents and advisers, Chairmen, Chief Executives and Technical Directors. If they existed at all, these roles used to be in the background but are now major public figures in their own right, some of them more influential than the manager or players. There is also an almost direct correlation between the wealth of a club's owner and their league position.

The 'slum sport' of the 1980s has re-invented itself, hugely successfully in purely monetary terms. The Premier League has become an international phenomenon, broadcast from state-of-the-art stadia where the paying customer enjoys the finest facilities, and paying wages which attract the world's best footballers. The game itself has benefitted from the application of sports science, improving conditioning, diet, fitness and kit. An emphasis on greater refereeing protection for players, the abolition of the back-pass rule (allowing the goalkeeper to pick up the ball from defenders) in 1992, and especially year-round perfect playing surfaces, have helped to create a new spectacle, at times faster-flowing and more technical than previously. In marketing and revenue-generation, the Premier League has led the way globally, with major European leagues following suit; the top tier is dominated by overseas owners, managers and players – its horizons are world-wide, and the lower divisions are left to fend for themselves. Its clubs undertake pre-season tours and friendlies in expanding markets across the globe rather than the traditional warm-ups against smaller teams around the British Isles.

English football's top clubs, aided by the FA and Sky, created a business model in the Premier League that excludes any meaningful form of wealth re-distribution throughout the League system – which will only continue to contract while the rich get richer, while television income continues to pour in at the highest level and its unprecedented wealth fails to 'trickle down' to those below. There has never been such a disparity within the English leagues, where transfer fees and wages reach ever-greater heights at the top while clubs are slowly squeezed out of existence at the bottom. The historical financial balances of regular transfers from the lower to the higher divisions, a generous percentage of TV deals, a designated share of gate money to the away team to reduce the advantage enjoyed by big-city clubs, are all but unknown in the Premier League era. Many clubs have effectively bankrupted themselves in their desperation to try and buy a place at the top table.

It is hard to imagine the gulf between the haves and the have-nots ever being bridged, as William McGregor's concept of a unified Football League disappears further into history with each passing season.

The Dell, Southampton (Southampton v Sunderland, FA Cup 1961/62). Courtesy of The Duncan Holley Collection.

The Dell, Southampton (Southampton v Charlton Athletic, Division Two 1965/66). Courtesy of The Duncan Holley Collection.

Burnden Park, Bolton (Bolton Wanderers v Blackburn Rovers, Division One 1960/61). Courtesy of David Williams.

*Before the Premier League*

Belle Vue, Doncaster (c. mid-1980s). © Steve McGhee.

Sealand Road, Chester (c. early-1990s). © Andy Dakin.

*Before the Premier League*

Goldstone Ground, Brighton (Brighton v Bradford City, Division Two 1984/85). © John Dewhirst.

Filbert Street, Leicester (Leicester City v Charlton Athletic, Division One 1986/87). © Peter Court, courtesy of James Court.

# English League Top Scorers 1958-92

### 1958/59
| | | | |
|---|---|---|---|
| Div 1 | Jimmy Greaves | Chelsea | 33 |
| Div 2 | Brian Clough | Middlesbrough | 42 |
| Div 3 | Jim Towers | Brentford | 32 |
| Div 4 | Arthur Rowley | Shrewsbury Town | 37 |

### 1959/60
| | | | |
|---|---|---|---|
| Div 1 | Dennis Viollet | Manchester United | 32 |
| Div 2 | Brian Clough | Middlesbrough | 39 |
| Div 3 | Derek Reeves | Southampton | 39 |
| Div 4 | Cliff Holton | Watford | 42 |

### 1960/61
| | | | |
|---|---|---|---|
| Div 1 | Jimmy Greaves | Chelsea | 41 |
| Div 2 | Ray Crawford | Ipswich Town | 39 |
| Div 3 | Tony Richards | Walsall | 36 |
| Div 4 | Terry Bly | Peterborough United | 52 |

### 1961/62
| | | | |
|---|---|---|---|
| Div 1 | Ray Crawford | Ipswich Town | 33 |
| | Derek Kevan | West Bromwich Albion | 33 |
| Div 2 | Roger Hunt | Liverpool | 41 |
| Div 3 | Cliff Holton | Watford/Northampton T | 37 |
| Div 4 | Bobby Hunt | Colchester United | 37 |

### 1962/63
| | | | |
|---|---|---|---|
| Div 1 | Jimmy Greaves | Tottenham Hotspur | 37 |
| Div 2 | Bobby Tambling | Chelsea | 35 |
| Div 3 | George Hudson | Coventry City | 30 |
| Div 4 | Ken Wagstaff | Mansfield Town | 34 |

### 1963/64
| | | | |
|---|---|---|---|
| Div 1 | Jimmy Greaves | Tottenham Hotspur | 35 |
| Div 2 | Ron Saunders | Portsmouth | 33 |
| Div 3 | Alfie Biggs | Bristol Rovers | 30 |
| Div 4 | Hugh McIlmoyle | Carlisle United | 39 |

## 1964/65

| | | | |
|---|---|---|---|
| Div 1 | Jimmy Greaves | Tottenham Hotspur | 29 |
| | Andy McEvoy | Blackburn Rovers | 29 |
| Div 2 | George O'Brien | Southampton | 34 |
| Div 3 | Ken Wagstaff | Mansfield T/Hull C | 35 |
| Div 4 | Alick Jeffrey | Doncaster Rovers | 36 |

## 1965/66

| | | | |
|---|---|---|---|
| Div 1 | Willie Irvine | Burnley | 29 |
| Div 2 | Martin Chivers | Southampton | 30 |
| Div 3 | Les Allen | Queens Park Rangers | 30 |
| Div 4 | Kevin Hector | Bradford Park Avenue | 44 |

## 1966/67

| | | | |
|---|---|---|---|
| Div 1 | Ron Davies | Southampton | 37 |
| Div 2 | Bobby Gould | Coventry City | 24 |
| Div 3 | Rodney Marsh | Queens Park Rangers | 30 |
| Div 4 | Ernie Phythian | Hartlepools United | 23 |

## 1967/68

| | | | |
|---|---|---|---|
| Div 1 | George Best | Manchester United | 28 |
| | Ron Davies | Southampton | 28 |
| Div 2 | John Hickton | Middlesbrough | 24 |
| Div 3 | Don Rogers | Swindon Town | 25 |
| Div 4 | Roy Chapman | Port Vale | 25 |
| | Les Massie | Halifax Town | 25 |

## 1968/69

| | | | |
|---|---|---|---|
| Div 1 | Jimmy Greaves | Tottenham Hotspur | 27 |
| Div 2 | John Toshack | Cardiff City | 22 |
| Div 3 | Don Rogers | Swindon Town | 22 |
| Div 4 | Gary Talbot | Chester | 22 |

## 1969/70

| | | | |
|---|---|---|---|
| Div 1 | Jeff Astle | West Bromwich Albion | 25 |
| Div 2 | John Hickton | Middlesbrough | 24 |
| Div 3 | George Jones | Bury | 26 |
| Div 4 | Albert Kinsey | Wrexham | 27 |

## 1970/71

| | | | |
|---|---|---|---|
| Div 1 | Tony Brown | West Bromwich Albion | 28 |
| Div 2 | John Hickton | Middlesbrough | 25 |
| Div 3 | Gerry Ingram | Preston North End | 22 |
| | Dudley Roberts | Mansfield Town | 22 |
| Div 4 | Ted MacDougall | Bournemouth | 42 |

## 1971-72

| | | | |
|---|---|---|---|
| Div 1 | Francis Lee | Manchester City | 33 |
| Div 2 | Bob Latchford | Birmingham City | 23 |
| Div 3 | Ted MacDougall | Bournemouth | 35 |
| Div 4 | Peter Price | Peterborough United | 28 |

## 1972/73

| | | | |
|---|---|---|---|
| Div 1 | Bryan 'Pop' Robson | West Ham United | 28 |
| Div 2 | Don Givens | Queens Park Rangers | 23 |
| Div 3 | Arthur Horsfield | Charlton Athletic | 26 |
| Div 4 | Fred Binney | Exeter City | 27 |

## 1973/74

| | | | |
|---|---|---|---|
| Div 1 | Mike Channon | Southampton | 21 |
| Div 2 | Duncan McKenzie | Nottingham Forest | 26 |
| Div 3 | Billy Jennings | Watford | 26 |
| Div 4 | Brian Yeo | Gillingham | 31 |

## 1974/75

| | | | |
|---|---|---|---|
| Div 1 | Malcolm MacDonald | Newcastle United | 21 |
| Div 2 | Brian Little | Aston Villa | 20 |
| Div 3 | Dixie McNeil | Hereford United | 31 |
| Div 4 | Ray Clarke | Mansfield Town | 28 |

## 1975/76

| | | | |
|---|---|---|---|
| Div 1 | Ted MacDougall | Norwich City | 23 |
| Div 2 | Derek Hales | Charlton Athletic | 28 |
| Div 3 | Dixie McNeil | Hereford United | 35 |
| Div 4 | Ronnie Moore | Tranmere Rovers | 34 |

### 1976/77

| | | | |
|---|---|---|---|
| Div 1 | Andy Gray | Aston Villa | 25 |
| | Malcolm MacDonald | Arsenal | 25 |
| Div 2 | Micky Walsh | Blackpool | 26 |
| Div 3 | Peter Ward | Brighton & Hove Albion | 32 |
| Div 4 | Brian Joicey | Barnsley | 25 |

### 1977/78

| | | | |
|---|---|---|---|
| Div 1 | Bob Latchford | Everton | 30 |
| Div 2 | Bob Hatton | Blackpool | 22 |
| Div 3 | Alex Bruce | Preston North End | 27 |
| Div 4 | Alan Curtis | Swansea City | 32 |
| | Steve Phillips | Brentford | 32 |

### 1978/79

| | | | |
|---|---|---|---|
| Div 1 | Frank Worthington | Bolton Wanderers | 24 |
| Div 2 | Bryan 'Pop' Robson | West Ham United | 24 |
| Div 3 | Ross Jenkins | Watford | 29 |
| Div 4 | John Dungworth | Aldershot | 26 |

### 1979/80

| | | | |
|---|---|---|---|
| Div 1 | Phil Boyer | Southampton | 23 |
| Div 2 | Clive Allen | Queens Park Rangers | 28 |
| Div 3 | Terry Curran | Sheffield Wednesday | 22 |
| Div 4 | Colin Garwood | Aldershot/Portsmouth | 27 |

### 1980/81

| | | | |
|---|---|---|---|
| Div 1 | Steve Archibald | Tottenham Hotspur | 20 |
| | Peter Withe | Aston Villa | 20 |
| Div 2 | David Cross | West Ham United | 22 |
| Div 3 | Tony Kellow | Exeter City | 25 |
| Div 4 | Alan Cork | Wimbledon | 23 |

### 1981/82

| | | | |
|---|---|---|---|
| Div 1 | Kevin Keegan | Southampton | 26 |
| Div 2 | Ronnie Moore | Rotherham United | 22 |
| Div 3 | Gordon Davies | Fulham | 24 |
| Div 4 | Keith Edwards | Hull C/Sheffield U | 36 |

**1982/83**

| | | | |
|---|---|---|---|
| Div 1 | Luther Blissett | Watford | 27 |
| Div 2 | Gary Lineker | Leicester City | 26 |
| Div 3 | Kerry Dixon | Reading | 26 |
| Div 4 | Steve Cammack | Scunthorpe United | 25 |

**1983/84**

| | | | |
|---|---|---|---|
| Div 1 | Ian Rush | Liverpool | 32 |
| Div 2 | Kerry Dixon | Chelsea | 28 |
| Div 3 | Keith Edwards | Sheffield United | 33 |
| Div 4 | Trevor Senior | Reading | 36 |

**1984/85**

| | | | |
|---|---|---|---|
| Div 1 | Kerry Dixon | Chelsea | 24 |
| | Gary Lineker | Leicester City | 24 |
| Div 2 | John Aldridge | Oxford United | 30 |
| Div 3 | Tommy Tynan | Plymouth Argyle | 31 |
| Div 4 | John Clayton | Tranmere Rovers | 31 |

**1985/86**

| | | | |
|---|---|---|---|
| Div 1 | Gary Lineker | Everton | 30 |
| Div 2 | Kevin Drinkell | Norwich City | 22 |
| Div 3 | Trevor Senior | Reading | 27 |
| Div 4 | Richard Cadette | Southend United | 25 |
| | Steve Taylor | Rochdale | 25 |

**1986/87**

| | | | |
|---|---|---|---|
| Div 1 | Clive Allen | Tottenham Hotspur | 33 |
| Div 2 | Mick Quinn | Portsmouth | 22 |
| Div 3 | Andy Jones | Port Vale | 29 |
| Div 4 | Richard Hill | Northampton Town | 28 |

**1987/88**

| | | | |
|---|---|---|---|
| Div 1 | John Aldridge | Liverpool | 26 |
| Div 2 | David Currie | Barnsley | 28 |
| Div 3 | David Crown | Southend United | 26 |
| Div 4 | Steve Bull | Wolverhampton W | 34 |

## 1988/89

| Div | Player | Club | Goals |
|---|---|---|---|
| Div 1 | Alan Smith | Arsenal | 23 |
| Div 2 | Keith Edwards | Hull City | 26 |
| Div 3 | Steve Bull | Wolverhampton W | 37 |
| Div 4 | Phil Stant | Hereford United | 28 |

## 1989/90

| Div | Player | Club | Goals |
|---|---|---|---|
| Div 1 | Gary Lineker | Tottenham Hotspur | 24 |
| Div 2 | Mick Quinn | Newcastle United | 32 |
| Div 3 | Bob Taylor | Bristol City | 27 |
| Div 4 | Brett Angell | Stockport County | 23 |

## 1990/91

| Div | Player | Club | Goals |
|---|---|---|---|
| Div 1 | Alan Smith | Arsenal | 22 |
| Div 2 | Teddy Sheringham | Millwall | 38 |
| Div 3 | Brett Angell | Southend United | 26 |
|  | Tony Philliskirk | Bolton Wanderers | 26 |
| Div 4 | Joe Allon | Hartlepool United | 35 |
|  | Steve Norris | Halifax Town | 35 |

## 1991/92

| Div | Player | Club | Goals |
|---|---|---|---|
| Div 1 | Ian Wright | Crystal Palace/Arsenal | 29 |
| Div 2 | Duncan Shearer | Swindon T/Blackburn R | 23 |
|  | David Speedie | Blackburn Rovers | 23 |
| Div 3 | Dean Holdsworth | Brentford | 24 |
| Div 4 | Dave Bamber | Blackpool | 26 |

# RECORDS

## Major English Records

### HIGHEST WINS

**Football League**

| | | | | |
|---|---|---|---|---|
| **Div 1 (Home)** | West Brom | 12-0 | Darwen | 04/04/1892 |
| | N Forest | 12-0 | Leicester Fosse | 21/04/1909 |
| **Div 1 (Away)** | Newcastle United | 1-9 | Sunderland | 05/12/1908 |
| | Cardiff City | 1-9 | Wolves | 03/09/1955 |
| **Div 2 (Home)** | Newcastle United | 13-0 | Newport County | 05/10/1946 |
| **Div 2 (Away)** | Burslem Port Vale | 0-10 | Sheffield United | 10/12/1892 |
| **Div 3 (Home)** | Gillingham | 10-0 | Chesterfield | 05/09/1987 |
| **Div 3 (Away)** | Halifax Town | 0-8 | Fulham | 16/09/1969 |
| **Div 3 (S) (Home)** | Luton Town | 12-0 | Bristol Rovers | 13/04/1936 |
| **Div 3 (S) (Away)** | Northampton Town | 0-8 | Walsall | 02/02/1947 |
| **Div 3 (N) (Home)** | Stockport County | 13-0 | Halifax Town | 06/01/1934 |
| **Div 3 (N) (Away)** | Accrington Stanley | 0-9 | Barnsley | 03/02/1934 |
| **Div 4 (Home)** | Oldham Athletic | 11-0 | Southport | 26/12/1962 |
| **Div 4 (Away)** | Crewe Alexandra | 1-8 | Rotherham United | 08/09/1973 |
| **Agg. Div 3 (N)** | Tranmere Rovers | 13-4 | Oldham Athletic | 26/12/1935 |

## Other

| | | | | |
|---|---|---|---|---|
| **Int'l** | England | 13-0 | Ireland | 18/02/1882 |
| **FA Cup** | Preston NE (*R1*) | 26-0 | Hyde United | 15/10/1887 |
| **Lge Cup** | West Ham (*R2, L2*) | 10-0 | Bury | 25/10/1983 |
| | Liverpool (*R2, L1*) | 10-0 | Fulham | 23/09/1986 |

## MOST GOALS FOR IN A SEASON

| | | Goals | Games | Season |
|---|---|---|---|---|
| **Div 1** | Aston Villa | 128 | 42 | 1930/31 |
| **Div 2** | Middlesbrough | 122 | 42 | 1926/27 |
| **Div 3 (N)** | Bradford City | 128 | 42 | 1928/29 |
| **Div 3 (S)** | Millwall | 127 | 42 | 1927/28 |
| **Div 3** | Queens Park Rangers | 111 | 46 | 1961/62 |
| **Div 4** | Peterborough United | 134 | 46 | 1960/61 |

## FEWEST GOALS FOR IN A SEASON
*(minimum 42 games)*

| | | Goals | Games | Season |
|---|---|---|---|---|
| **Div 1** | Stoke City | 24 | 42 | 1984/85 |
| **Div 2** | Watford | 24 | 42 | 1971/72 |
| **Div 3 (N)** | Crewe Alexandra | 32 | 42 | 1923/24 |
| **Div 3 (S)** | Crystal Palace | 33 | 42 | 1950/51 |
| **Div 3** | Stockport County | 27 | 46 | 1969/70 |
| **Div 4** | Crewe Alexandra | 29 | 46 | 1981/82 |

## MOST GOALS AGAINST IN A SEASON

|          |                    | Goals | Games | Season  |
|----------|--------------------|-------|-------|---------|
| Div 1    | Blackpool          | 125   | 42    | 1930/31 |
| Div 2    | Darwen             | 141   | 34    | 1898/99 |
| Div 3 (N)| Nelson             | 136   | 42    | 1927/28 |
| Div 3 (S)| Merthyr Tydfil     | 135   | 42    | 1929/30 |
| Div 3    | Accrington Stanley | 123   | 46    | 1959/60 |
| Div 4    | Hartlepools United | 109   | 46    | 1959/60 |

## FEWEST GOALS AGAINST IN A SEASON
*(minimum 42 games)*

|          |                   | Goals | Games | Season  |
|----------|-------------------|-------|-------|---------|
| Div 1    | Liverpool         | 16    | 42    | 1978/79 |
| Div 2    | Manchester United | 23    | 42    | 1924/25 |
| Div 3 (N)| Port Vale         | 21    | 46    | 1953/54 |
| Div 3 (S)| Southampton       | 21    | 42    | 1921/22 |
| Div 3    | Middlesbrough     | 30    | 46    | 1986/87 |
| Div 4    | Lincoln City      | 25    | 46    | 1980/81 |

## MOST POINTS IN A SEASON
*(two points for a win)*

|          |                   | Points | Games | Season  |
|----------|-------------------|--------|-------|---------|
| Div 1    | Liverpool         | 68     | 42    | 1978/79 |
| Div 2    | Tottenham Hotspur | 70     | 42    | 1919/20 |
| Div 3 (N)| Doncaster Rovers  | 72     | 42    | 1946/47 |
| Div 3 (S)| Nottingham Forest | 70     | 46    | 1950/51 |
|          | Bristol City      | 70     | 46    | 1954/55 |
| Div 3    | Aston Villa       | 70     | 46    | 1971/72 |
| Div 4    | Lincoln City      | 74     | 46    | 1975/76 |

## MOST POINTS IN A SEASON
*(three points for a win)*

|  |  | Points | Games | Season |
|---|---|---|---|---|
| **Div 1** | Everton | 90 | 42 | 1984/85 |
|  | Liverpool | 90 | 40 | 1987/88 |
| **Div 2** | Chelsea | 99 | 46 | 1988/89 |
| **Div 3** | Bournemouth | 97 | 46 | 1986/87 |
| **Div 4** | Swindon Town | 102 | 46 | 1985/86 |

## FEWEST POINTS IN A SEASON
*(minimum 34 games)*

|  |  | Points | Games | Season |
|---|---|---|---|---|
| **Div 1** | Stoke City | 17 | 42 | 1984/85 |
| **Div 2** | Doncaster Rovers | 8 | 34 | 1904/05 |
|  | Loughborough Town | 8 | 34 | 1899/1900 |
| **Div 3 (N)** | Rochdale | 11 | 40 | 1931/32 |
| **Div 3 (S)** | Merthyr Tydfil | 21 | 42 | 1924/25 & 1929/30 |
|  | Queens Park Rangers | 21 | 42 | 1925/26 |
| **Div 3** | Rochdale | 21 | 46 | 1973/74 |
|  | Cambridge United | 21 | 46 | 1984/85 |
| **Div 4** | Workington | 19 | 46 | 1976/77 |

## MOST WINS IN A SEASON

|  |  | Wins | Games | Season |
|---|---|---|---|---|
| **Div 1** | Tottenham Hotspur | 31 | 42 | 1960/61 |
| **Div 2** | Tottenham Hotspur | 32 | 42 | 1919/20 |
| **Div 3 (N)** | Doncaster Rovers | 33 | 42 | 1946/47 |
| **Div 3 (S)** | Millwall | 30 | 42 | 1927/28 |
|  | Plymouth Argyle | 30 | 42 | 1929/30 |
|  | Cardiff City | 30 | 42 | 1946/47 |
|  | Nottingham Forest | 30 | 46 | 1950/51 |
|  | Bristol City | 30 | 46 | 1954/55 |
| **Div 3** | Aston Villa | 32 | 46 | 1971/72 |
| **Div 4** | Lincoln City | 32 | 46 | 1975/76 |
|  | Swindon Town | 32 | 46 | 1985/86 |

## MOST DRAWN GAMES IN A SEASON

|  |  | Draws | Games | Season |
|---|---|---|---|---|
| **Div 1** | Norwich City | 23 | 42 | 1978/79 |
| **Div 4** | Exeter City | 23 | 46 | 1986/87 |

## FEWEST WINS IN A SEASON

|  |  | Wins | Games | Season |
|---|---|---|---|---|
| **Div 1** | Stoke | 3 | 22 | 1889/90 |
|  | Woolwich Arsenal | 3 | 38 | 1912/13 |
|  | Stoke City | 3 | 42 | 1984/85 |
| **Div 2** | Loughborough T | 1 | 34 | 1899/1900 |
| **Div 3 (N)** | Rochdale | 4 | 40 | 1931/32 |
| **Div 3 (S)** | Merthyr Tydfil | 6 | 42 | 1929/30 |
|  | Queens Park Rangers | 6 | 42 | 1925/26 |
| **Div 3** | Rochdale | 2 | 46 | 1973/74 |
| **Div 4** | Southport | 3 | 46 | 1976/77 |

## MOST DEFEATS IN A SEASON

| Div 1 | Stoke City | 31 | 42 | 1984/85 |
|---|---|---|---|---|
| Div 2 | Tranmere Rovers | 31 | 42 | 1938/39 |
| Div 3 (N) | Rochdale | 33 | 40 | 1931/32 |
| Div 3 (S) | Merthyr Tydfil | 29 | 42 | 1924/25 |
| | Walsall | 29 | 46 | 1952/53 & 1953/54 |
| Div 3 | Cambridge United | 33 | 46 | 1984/85 |
| Div 4 | Newport County | 33 | 46 | 1987/88 |

## FEWEST DEFEATS IN A SEASON
*(minimum 20 games)*

| | | Defeats | Games | Season |
|---|---|---|---|---|
| Div 1 | Preston North End | 0 | 22 | 1888/89 |
| | Arsenal | 1 | 38 | 1990/91 |
| | Liverpool | 2 | 40 | 1987/88 |
| | Leeds United | 2 | 42 | 1968/69 |
| Div 2 | Liverpool | 0 | 28 | 1893/94 |
| | Burnley | 2 | 30 | 1897/98 |
| | Bristol City | 2 | 38 | 1905/06 |
| | Leeds United | 3 | 42 | 1963/64 |
| Div 3 (N) | Port Vale | 3 | 46 | 1953/54 |
| | Doncaster Rovers | 3 | 42 | 1946/47 |
| | Wolverhampton W | 3 | 42 | 1923/24 |
| Div 3 (S) | Southampton | 4 | 42 | 1921/22 |
| | Plymouth Argyle | 4 | 42 | 1929/30 |
| Div 3 | Q.P.R. | 5 | 46 | 1966/67 |
| | Bristol Rovers | 5 | 46 | 1989/90 |
| Div 4 | Lincoln City | 4 | 46 | 1975/76 |
| | Sheffield United | 4 | 46 | 1981/82 |
| | Bournemouth | 4 | 46 | 1981/82 |

## LONGEST WINNING SEQUENCE

|  |  | Games | Season |
|---|---|---|---|
| **Div 1** | Everton | 12 | 1893/94 & 1894/95 |
| **Div 2** | Manchester United | 14 | 1904/05 |
|  | Bristol City | 14 | 1905/06 |
|  | Preston North End | 14 | 1950/51 |
| **Div 3** | Reading | 13 | 1985/86 |

## Individual

### MOST GOALS IN A SEASON

|  |  | Goals | Games | Season |
|---|---|---|---|---|
| **Div 1** | Dixie Dean (Everton) | 60 | 39 | 1927/28 |
| **Div 2** | George Camsell (Middlesbrough) | 59 | 37 | 1926/27 |
| **Div 3 (N)** | Ted Harston (Mansfield Town) | 55 | 41 | 1936/37 |
| **Div 3 (S)** | Joe Payne (Luton Town) | 55 | 39 | 1936/37 |
| **Div 3** | Derek Reeves (Southampton) | 39 | 46 | 1959/60 |
| **Div 4** | Terry Bly (Peterborough Utd) | 52 | 46 | 1960/61 |
| **FA Cup** | Sandy Brown (Tottenham Hotspur) | 15 |  | 1900/01 |
| **Lge Cup** | Clive Allen (Tottenham Hotspur) | 12 |  | 1986/87 |

## MOST GOALS IN A GAME

|  |  | Goals | Date |
|---|---|---|---|
| D. 1 | Ted Drake (Aston Villa v **Arsenal**) | 7 | 14/12/1935 |
| D. 2 | Tommy Briggs (**Blackburn Rovers** v Bristol Rovers) | 7 | 05/02/1955 |
|  | Tim Coleman (**Stoke City** v Lincoln City) | 7 | 23/02/1957 |
| D. 3 (N) | Bunny Bell (**Tranmere Rovers** v Oldham Athletic) | 9 | 26/12/1935 |
| D. 3 (S) | Joe Payne (**Luton Town** v Bristol Rovers) | 10 | 13/04/1936 |
| D. 3 | Tony Caldwell (**Bolton Wanderers** v Walsall) | 5 | 10/09/1983 |
|  | Keith East (**Swindon Town** v Mansfield Town) | 5 | 20/11/1965 |
|  | Steve Earle (Halifax Town v **Fulham**) | 5 | 16/09/1969 |
|  | Andy Jones (**Port Vale** v Newport County) | 5 | 04/05/1987 |
|  | Barrie Thomas (**Scunthorpe United** v Luton Town) | 5 | 24/04/1965 |
|  | Steve Wilkinson (**Mansfield Town** v Birmingham City) | 5 | 03/04/1990 |
|  | Alf Wood (**Shrewsbury Town** v Blackburn Rovers) | 5 | 02/10/1971 |
| D. 4 | Bert Lister (**Oldham Athletic** v Southport) | 6 | 26/12/1962 |
| FA Cup | Ted MacDougall (**Bournemouth** v Margate, R1) | 9 | 20/11/1971 |
| Lge Cup | Frank Bunn (**Oldham Athletic** v Scarborough, R3) | 6 | 25/10/1989 |

# Individual Player & Club Records

## Players with over 300 Football League Goals

*Arthur Rowley* – 434*, 1946-64: West Bromwich Albion (4), Fulham (27), Leicester City (251), Shrewsbury Town (152)

*Dixie Dean* – 379, 1923-38: Notts County (3), Everton (349), Tranmere Rovers (27)

*Jimmy Greaves* – 357^, 1957-70: Chelsea (124), Tottenham Hotspur (220), West Ham United (13)

*Steve Bloomer* – 352, 1892-1913: Derby County (240), Middlesbrough (59), Derby County (53)

*George Camsell* – 345, 1924-39: Durham City (20), Middlesbrough (325)

*John Atyeo* – 315, 1950-65: Bristol City (315)

*Joe Smith* – 315, 1908-28: Bolton Wanderers (254), Stockport County (61)

*Vic Watson* – 312, 1920-36: West Ham United (298), Southampton (14)

*Harry Bedford* – 308, 1919-34: Nottingham Forest, Blackpool, Derby County, Newcastle United, Sunderland, Bradford Park Avenue, Chesterfield

*Harry Johnson* – 307, 1919-35: Sheffield United (201), Mansfield Town (106)

Honourable Mention: *John Aldridge* – 213+ (330 in total), 1979-98: Newport County (70), Oxford United (72), Liverpool (50), Tranmere Rovers (138)

---

*Some sources show Arthur Rowley's total as being 433 goals
^ Jimmy Greaves also scored 9 goals for AC Milan
+ John Aldridge also scored 33 goals for Real Sociedad

## Players with over 750 Football League Appearances [to 1992]

*Peter Shilton* – 968, 1966-92 (1005 in total, to 1997): Leicester City (286), Stoke City (110), Nottingham Forest (202), Southampton (188), Derby County (175), Plymouth Argyle (7)
*Terry Paine* – 824, 1957-1977: Southampton (713), Hereford United (111)
*Tommy Hutchison* – 795, 1968-1991: Blackpool (165), Coventry City (314), Manchester City (46), Burnley (92), Swansea City (178)
*Alan Oakes* – 776, 1959-1983: Manchester City (564), Chester City (211), Port Vale (1)
*John Trollope* – 770, 1960-1980: Swindon Town (770)
*Jimmy Dickinson* – 764, 1946-1967: Portsmouth (764)
*Roy Sproson* – 761, 1950-1972: Port Vale (761)
*Billy Bonds* – 758, 1964-1988: Charlton Athletic (95), West Ham United (663)
*Ray Clemence* – 758, 1965-1987: Scunthorpe United (48), Liverpool (470), Tottenham Hotspur (240)
*Pat Jennings* – 757, 1963-1985: Watford (48), Tottenham Hotspur (472), Arsenal (237)
*Frank Worthington* – 757, 1966-1988: Huddersfield Town (171), Leicester City (210), Bolton Wanderers (84), Birmingham City (75), Leeds United (32), Sunderland (19), Southampton (34), Brighton & Hove Albion (31), Tranmere Rovers (59), Preston North End (23), Stockport County (19)
*Robbie James* – 751, 1973-1992 (782 in total, to 1993): Swansea City (484), Stoke City (48), Queens Park Rangers (87), Leicester City (23), Bradford City (89), Cardiff City (51)

## Honourable Mentions [pre- and post- 1992]:

*Tony Ford* – 931, 1975-2001: Grimsby Town (423), Sunderland (9), Stoke City (112), West Bromwich Albion (114), Bradford City (5), Scunthorpe United (76), Mansfield Town (103), Rochdale (89)
*Graham Alexander* – 833, 1991-2012: Scunthorpe United (159), Luton Town (150), Preston North End (370), Burnley (154)

*Neil Redfearn* – 790, 1982-2004: Bolton Wanderers (35), Lincoln City (100), Doncaster Rovers (46), Crystal Palace (57), Watford (24), Oldham Athletic (62), Barnsley (292), Charlton Athletic (30), Bradford City (17), Wigan Athletic (22), Halifax Town (42), Boston United (54), Rochdale (9)

*David James* – 788, 1990-2013: Watford (89), Liverpool (214), Aston Villa (67), West Ham United (91), Manchester City (93), Portsmouth (134), Bristol City (81), AFC Bournemouth (19)

*Dave Beasant* – 773, 1980-2003: Wimbledon (340), Newcastle United (20), Chelsea (133), Grimsby Town (6), Wolverhampton Wanderers (4), Southampton (88), Nottingham Forest (139), Portsmouth (27), Brighton & Hove Albion (16)

*Mick Tait* – 761, 1974-1997: Oxford United (64), Carlisle United (106), Hull City (33), Portsmouth (241), Reading (99), Darlington (79), Hartlepool United (139)

*Wayne Allison* – 752, 1987-2008: Halifax Town (84), Watford (7), Bristol City (195), Swindon Town (101), Huddersfield Town (74), Tranmere Rovers (103), Sheffield United (73), Chesterfield (115)

**Consecutive Football League Appearances:** Harold Bell – 401, Tranmere Rovers (1946-55)

\*\*\*

**League Championship Hat-Tricks**
Huddersfield Town, 1923/24 to 1925/26
Arsenal, 1932/33 to 1934/35
Liverpool, 1981/82 to 1983/84

**Record Home Wins in a season:** Brentford won all 21 games in Division 3 (S), 1929/30

**Record Away Wins in a season:** Doncaster Rovers won 18 of 21 games in Division 3 (N), 1946/47

**Undefeated at Home (Sequence):** Liverpool, 85 games (63 League, 9 League Cup, 7 European, 6 FA Cup) Jan 1978-Jan 1981

**Longest Winning Sequence from season's start:** Tottenham Hotspur, 11 games, 1960/61 (Division 1)

**Longest Sequence without a win in a season:** Cambridge United, 31 games, 1983/84 (Division 2)

**Longest Sequence without a win from season's start:** Sheffield United, 16 games, 1990/91 (Division 1)

**Longest Sequence of consecutive defeats:** Darwen, 18 games, 1898/99 (Division 2)

**Longest Sequence of consecutive scoring:** 15 (in 12 games) – Bill Prendergast (Chester, 1938/39)

**Longest Unbeaten Sequence:** Nottingham Forest, 42 games, Nov 1977-Dec 1978 (Division 1)

**Longest Unbeaten Sequence in a season:** Burnley, 30 games, 1920/21 (Division 1)

**Longest Unbeaten Cup Sequence:** Liverpool, 25 Rounds, League/Milk Cup 1980-84

**Longest Unbeaten Sequence from season's start:** Leeds United, 29 games, 1973/74 (Division 1); Liverpool, 29 games, 1987/88 (Division 1)

**Hat-Tricks**
*Career:* Dixie Dean – 37 (Tranmere Rovers, Everton, Notts County, England)
*Division One (one season, post-war):* Jimmy Greaves – 6 (Chelsea, 1960-61)

**Consecutive Goals in Football League Games:** 12, Jimmy Dunne, for Sheffield United between 24 October 1931 and 1 January 1932, a total of 18 goals (Division 1); 12, Dixie Dean for Everton between 6 December 1930 and 18 February 1931, a total of 23 goals (Division 2).

**Fastest League Goal:** 4 seconds – Jim Fryatt, *Bradford Park Avenue* v Tranmere Rovers, 25 April 1964 (Division 4)

**Goalkeeper: Longest Period without conceding a Football League goal:** Steve Death, Reading, 1,103 minutes from 24 March to 18 August 1979

**Most Football League Championship Medals:** 8 – Phil Neal, Liverpool (1975/76, 1976/77, 1978/79, 1979/80, 1981/82, 1982/83, 1983/84, 1985/86)

**Youngest Football League Players:** Albert Geldard, 15 years 158 days (Millwall v *Bradford Park Avenue*, Division 2, 16 September 1929) & Ken Roberts, 15 years 158 days (Bradford Park Avenue v *Wrexham*, Division 3 (N), 1 September 1951)

**Oldest Football League Player:** Neil McBain, 52 years 4 months (Hartlepools United v *New Brighton*, Division 3 (N), 15 March 1947)

# Interviews

I have included a section of interviews with players, fans and historians to give first-hand perspectives on English league football in the years before the Premier League. All of them kindly gave their time to share memories and stories of the game, spanning over half a century. Their experiences bring to life many of the topics discussed earlier in the book, from people who played and watched the English game at all levels of the Football League over the decades before 1992. The following were interviewed; all interviews were conducted in 2020 and early 2021.

Gavin Buckland
Keith Buxton
Paul Davis
Ron Futcher
Nigel Gleghorn
Derek Goodier
Steve Hetzke
Rick Holden
Gerry Stewart

# Gavin Buckland

Gavin is Everton's official statistician, *A Question of Sport* script consultant, *Radio Merseyside* regular, and *Liverpool Echo* 'Royal Blue' podcaster. He is the author of several books including *Money Can't Buy Us Love: Everton in the 1960s* and *Everton, Strange but Blue: Moments That Shocked and Surprised the Fans*.

***What are your earliest football memories – can you remember a particular game on TV, or a match you went to?***

I'm from the generation that the first time they probably saw a game of football in colour was when they actually went to the game. So my first game was 1972 but we had a black and white television at the time. My first football memories in terms of actually watching a game would be early '72 – watching Everton on *Match of the Day* against Arsenal, 1st January 1972; when they'd just sold Alan Ball to Highbury. Like most of my generation, the first I knew of football, the way I was introduced to it, was football cards. That was the gateway to knowing players and teams. I was only 5 or 6 and didn't read newspapers or such, so I found out through collecting football cards. That would be my first source of knowledge about the game and then, naturally from that, quite early in 1972, I started getting *Shoot!* magazine every week – it was always *Shoot!* or *Goal.*

[On TV] It was just *Match of the Day* really, and Sunday afternoons on Granada television – the glorious and sadly never-replaced regional highlights show. There was certainly something lost in '83 when they removed regional highlights shows, it went to more of a corporate feel. That was it really, started watching games on the telly, first World Cup was '74, first World Cup involving England was '82. It was quite funny actually. We had an 'O' Level exam at school but because England were playing they started and finished quarter of an hour early, so I left the exam and ran home to watch the first England World Cup game I'd ever seen; got in after a minute and they'd already scored! I waited 16 years to see England score a goal in a World Cup, and I missed it...

In Liverpool, like all major cities, when you were young football was all you had, you didn't have anything else. Certainly in the winter, it was the sole activity, playing it or talking about it, or watching it. Liverpool being such a two-club city, and Everton were still a massive club at the time, before Liverpool started taking off in the mid-70s, winning European Cups, it was still very much equal. I'd listen to Radio 2, local radio if Everton were playing and like a lot of people, certainly by the mid-70s, Radio 2 was the thing midweek, listening to big European games. The first European Cup Final I saw was '72, first international game I saw was England 1 West Germany 3 at Wembley, April 1972 [European Championship quarter-final], which was great.

So watching the European Championship in '72, [West] Germany, fantastic – Barry Davies said it was the best international team he'd seen, certainly one of the top three and the best German team I've seen, and there's been some great ones. My interest waned a bit in the late 70s for the simple reason I went to school and I was doing sports. Cricket was always my big sport, but 1980/81 I started going again.

When you're a teenager, it's slightly different, that togetherness and bonding, when you start to feel part of a crowd – even when gates were 15,000 [at Goodison Park], it's still a lot of people to be in close proximity to. You start to understand the relationship between you and the club a little better. It wasn't like now, the Internet-driven stuff, clubs as content providers. If you look at matchday programmes 40 years ago, they were the news of the club – far more informative, not selling the brand like they are now. The club didn't go out of its way to forge a relationship with supporters; you never got the impression that the club would make a decision to satisfy the fans. It was still very much a 'them and us,' which I actually think is quite healthy – it can be too close now, I think. In the mid-80s there was a healthy distance between the two. There's the obvious stuff of feeling closer to the players – when you see the match programmes, say 1986, and you've got those Q and A's, and the question is about 'my dream car.' This is First Division footballers, really well paid! I'd like to know at what point they took that question out as redundant. Those questions are fascinating commentaries on the state of the game at the time, perfect for the mid-80s.

By the early 80s, *Match of the Day* and *The Big Match,* which were massive events in the 70s, had lost their lustre – familiarity meant they were no longer event television, especially when they started moving them around. They had millions of viewers in the 70s, but by the 80s there were two things – a decline in people wanting to watch football, and also they were a bit outmoded, and the general feeling was that they wanted live football.

From the 1960s you could see a change in the way the game was covered in newspapers, tabloids just gave you the bog-standard reports and results – it was only really someone like Ken Jones in the *Mirror*, his Monday column commentary pieces, they were way ahead of the game in the late 60s/early 70s. I'd never seen that before. The growth of the tabloid Sunday newspapers in the 60s, they could devote more pages to football than the dailies, and that's when they started filling it with transfer gossip, which you never used to get. It wasn't just speculation, the clubs deliberately planted stories. Alan Ball had a big argument with Harry Catterick in late August/early September 1971 and two weeks later there was a story in the *Sunday People*, 'Alan Ball may be leaving Everton' – that wasn't a coincidence! A lot of it wasn't like the gossip you get now, it was given by clubs or agents to generate interest – you didn't have the Internet, and contact between clubs was limited, they only had the [transfer] list they put out now and again.

### *Who were your favourite players, growing up?*

There was a dearth of football on television, so the chances of being influenced by players from other teams was limited – you'd only see them a couple of times a season. When I was younger I saw Gunter Netzer playing at Wembley for Germany in 1972 [see above] in the old European Nations Cup quarter-final at Wembley. Netzer was fantastic, a real influence and I spent most of the summer of 1972 trying to copy him on the street! Lots of people were really affected by that performance, but you may not see him play again. Some obvious ones, Johan Cruyff for Holland and Ajax in the early 70s when I was growing up, George Best, Gordon Banks but other First Division clubs, you'd hardly ever see them. Once or twice on *Match of the Day*, televised highlights, because ITV in the north-west, you only saw the same teams over and over again. Your access to football on television was just far less. I don't remember having a favourite player from another English team, maybe favourite England players – by the mid-70s, '77, I always liked the two Man United wingers, Gordon Hill and Steve Coppell. They were quite entertaining. Access was just so limited, you might get a bit in *On the Ball* or *Football Focus*, but it wasn't like now.

***What were your impressions of attending games before the Premier League era – the atmosphere, the facilities at the stadiums?***

Going to games in the early-mid-80s, a major thing was hooliganism – I didn't really notice it on Merseyside because it was such a well-controlled environment, which it needed to be. You were always conscious of it, fans being kept in after the game, walks from the train station to the ground. You just took it as read, part of the game, even with the relatively small crowds. Racism – yes, absolutely – I was there when someone behind Alex Williams [Manchester City goalkeeper] dressed as a Ku Klux Klan in 1982, but again it was part of the game, you don't realise the implications of it. When I look back on it now, more should have been done, but I'm a big believer in what Arthur Hopcraft [author of *The Football Man*] says, football being a reflection of wider society, and it wasn't being tackled there. Merseyside was particularly nasty.

Terraces, fences, you also took as read, they'd been doing that for time immemorial so you didn't realise that fences were at some point a health risk, as we well know. I think that was all due to your sole experience of supporting the club was watching a game of football. There was very little information, maybe the newspapers, but you judged the club by what you were seeing on matchday, not really bothered about facilities – you just grew up with them. I remember watching the odd game in the stand, but it never felt like a massive step up, you were just sitting down rather than standing up. I went on the Kop a few times in the 80s to watch big games, and it happened with Everton as well, looking back on it now the crush of the crowd, it's quite scary. Crush barriers weren't great, you could go down the terraces quite quickly.

I think every match-going supporter, anyone who had been in a tightly-packed English football ground in the 70s and 80s, knew that Hillsborough was an accident just waiting to happen. Something similar happened to me outside Villa Park before the FA Cup semi-final in 1986 [Everton v Sheffield Wednesday].

***With the improvements in safety and facilities, would you say there's been any trade-off, anything lost from the experience of attending games in the 1970s and 80s?***

Not really in terms of a watching experience, it's still possible to feel part of a crowd when you're sitting down. I suppose the one thing that has been lost is a minor thing; freedom in the ground. I used to go in the enclosure at Everton, so attacking the Park End first half. I'd stand at that end, and then move to the Gwladys Street end for the second half. When you see games on television, you'd see whichever end Everton were attacking would be chocka! So freedom of movement inside the ground to a degree, but not a lot really as an experience – you've seen some great atmospheres at Goodison, like other grounds, to match anything in the 70s and 80s, in a seating environment.

***Did you notice any major differences between the divisions of the Football League in the 1970s and 80s?***

The first thing you noticed – and you had a lot of coverage, that was one of the benefits of regional telly, even *Match of the Day* was contracted to show lower division games – individual players might be better, but no difference in terms of the spectacle. I think there's a number of reasons, firstly money runs the game and you didn't have that gap, foreign players etc, and secondly then the rules of the game and the pitches were a great equaliser. The rules now encourage more skilful players, tactics, better managers made that gap enormous, and it's not just money.

You wouldn't notice that much difference then. If you played a lower division team in the Cup, they had their strongest team out, especially away from home there was always a possibility of getting beat. The one game I think that sums that up is when Sunderland beat Leeds in the 1973 FA Cup Final – Leeds, such a massive team, great names, Sunderland were the underdogs, Second Division but you look at that team and they'd got some top players. Dennis Tueart, Dave Watson with 60-odd caps for England, Jim Montgomery who was a very good goalkeeper, Billy Hughes, Ian Porterfield – all good players, but they were huge underdogs. It was a major shock. I don't think games like that exist any more.

That's one of the big changes, the demise of the FA Cup. It hasn't helped itself over the years. Unfortunately this is probably one of the by-products of Hillsborough, but I think you can trace it to the broadcast of the live games [semi-finals] in '90 – that was just about manageable, but not when it went to Wembley with Spurs-Arsenal in '91. Ever since then, there's been a number of step changes in the Cup, quite apart from the wider issue of the difference in wealth, and every change has been to the detriment of it for the last 30 years. Scrapping the second replay, spreading live coverage over the weekend, the Man United thing in 1999/2000, the general escalation in wealth, foreign players coming in who don't appreciate its heritage – and younger supporters who don't, and the number of live games. Even in 1990, the FA Cup Final was still a big live event because there were still only about 10-20 games shown live. Once the Premier League started and you had about 60 live games, the FA Cup was just another game. So all of those things over the years have contributed to the demise of the FA Cup, which is sad but inevitable – I just don't think they've done anything to pull that back.

What I would say is how massive the FA Cup Final was in English football, and English culture, it stood out above anything else in sport. [In the 70s] There'd only be three live games – the Cup Final, England-Scotland and the European Cup Final – so it was just a massive occasion. So some of the earliest memories are built around FA Cup Finals, '72 was the first one I saw, then '73 Leeds-Sunderland stands out, we've talked about it earlier. As a younger fan, some of your favourites might come from the Cup Final – it went way beyond football, by a country mile the biggest sporting event [in the UK].

That's another thing, foreign players, which was still relatively slow. Ardiles and Villa was '78, when they lifted the [overseas transfer] rules, but even in '92 there were only eight or nine in the Premier League, on the opening day. English football was still insular. I remember it was a massive thing, when Ardiles and Villa were bought, first game away to Forest. Such a big story, both foreign, both from Argentina when they'd just won the World Cup. Even in the 80s though, it wasn't a big thing – Everton didn't have a foreign player until the late 80s – not a big part of the culture. Top teams, Liverpool had Molby, a great player, but clubs still had the core of their team from England, Scotland, Wales, Northern Ireland. So I'd say foreign players have changed English football, but not necessarily in that thirty-year span [50s to 80s] that we're talking about. Ardiles was still probably the best known, and the other two would be Muhren and Thijssen, but overall, nowhere near the influence they have now. You wonder if some were put off by playing in the English game then.

Also, English clubs in Europe was always such a big thing – Wednesday nights, you didn't have live games, but there'd be five or six clubs playing, on Radio 2. The English clubs would be supported by most of the people in England – unless it was a rival, like Everton with Liverpool! They were still seen as England's representatives, less partisan times, and a club winning the European Cup was a national celebration. One I always remember was Aberdeen winning the Cup Winners' Cup [in 1983], everyone was made up! It's interesting to think when it changed – the Heysel ban, obviously, but when you get to the Premier League era, and the Champions League with more than one team, so they're no longer that country's representative, it's different. That's another change, the general attitude of supporters towards English clubs in Europe. Heysel changed it as well, I think there was still a bit of bitterness over Liverpool.

A couple of things about Heysel: a) I could see why the authorities had become so frustrated with English football, that they needed to do something about it. Not just Heysel, there was a long history of trouble. I could understand it, but whether banning indefinitely or five years was right? You knew there was a ban coming, but five years was harsh. b) the one thing I didn't get is, if they wanted to stop hooliganism abroad, ban the national team then. If that's what they wanted to avoid, there'd been more serious trouble with England – in Spain '82, in Italy '80 – so if you're thinking that the behaviour of football fans abroad is damaging the reputation of football in this country, then ban the national team. I'm surprised that wasn't picked up on more at the time. Hooliganism abroad did damage the reputation of the country.

The ban affected English football though – Everton played a European final two weeks before Heysel, in Rotterdam, and the fans behaved impeccably. So it was harsh, and I do wonder if that started to affect the partisan attitude we've got today. I understand that they couldn't just let that happen, and I get that Thatcher was attacking the working class, but I just think it was a case of 'remove the people, remove the problem.' You maybe had to be around at the time to appreciate why they did it.

I think the 80s in many respects are a lost decade for English football, and that's because of how history works. By the time the Premier League had started, the 80s history hadn't really been written because it was so recent (the 70s had to a degree). Then when the Premier League started, it generated its own history and there was no need to revisit the 80s, or even the late 70s. It's fallen through the gaps in the floorboards as a consequence – it was almost too recent to be part of Football League history, but fell outside of Premier League history. That meant not just the likes of Everton's title-winning teams were missed off, but Arsenal under George Graham, two titles. Leeds won the title in '92, Blackburn in '95 – only three years difference – people still talk about Blackburn, but never that Leeds team. They may as well be 300 years apart, the amount of coverage they've got over the last 25 years! I do think it's that pre-Premier League history – Liverpool get recalled because they were part of the Anfield dynasty that stretched back twenty years before but Forest, Villa get forgotten – fifteen years from the late 70s to the early 90s, it's a bit of a vacuum. As though it's not old enough to be part of English football's heritage, but it's not the Premier League either.

The other peculiar thing which you don't get now, particularly in the 80s, was that phenomenon of supporters picking and choosing their games. You can see at clubs like

Manchester City or Arsenal, from the late 70s to the end of the 80s, they might get 20,000 for the game before the derby, and then when it's Manchester United or Tottenham, it'll be 55,000. The support was still out there, but they weren't turning up every week, for lots of reasons – hooliganism, the economy.

## Did football start to change in the general culture around Italia '90?

It's hard to imagine now the way that football was regarded in the early-to-mid-80s – if you said you were a football fan, you may as well have been a drunk driver in terms of social impact. That was reflected in the popularity of the game, and the popularity of footballers – in the mid-80s, the most popular sportspeople in England would be athletes, cricketers and snooker players. Footballers were way down the pecking order, Bryan Robson was England captain, but he wasn't that famous compared to David Gower or Ian Botham, he wasn't a celebrity. There was no cross-over into popular culture. So as a football fan, you were a pariah, and that was down to hooliganism, the economic recession and crumbling stadia. The game wasn't particularly well run, we were paying for the lack of investment in the game in the 70s.

I think 85/86 was the lowest attendances of any season, before it picked up again – and there was a moment before Italia '90; in the 88/89 season when you saw the literal growth of inflatables at grounds, and it brought a little bit of humour to the game that had not been there for many, many years. Teenage culture was changing as well, it was good to see that humour in football. So I think before Italia '90 there were just small signs – you also had the 1989 Liverpool-Arsenal League Championship game, live audience on a Friday night before a Bank Holiday, you'd kill for that now. 88/89, you had Hillsborough in there, but that Arsenal game was a big pointer to how football would be televised; it showed that live football was an event that people would watch, and how it would operate as a business.

Italia '90 was undoubtedly the poorest international tournament I've ever seen – equal with Euro '96 – the two best tournaments for England in my lifetime, but awful football. But Italia '90 in culture – yes. You had the New Order song, 'World in Motion,' and I doubt if there's ever been a more important influence on the culture in any sphere of entertainment – and Gascoigne. I think without Italia '90, you may still have got the Premier League, but a watered-down version. A massive long-term cultural influence on this country. It became a little more acceptable to be a football fan, almost fashionable.

*What were the most memorable games you went to, before the Premier League?*

I think one of them would be the first time I went to Wembley, and that goes back to the FA Cup Final being this massive event, and when Wembley only staged two or three club games a season, so there was a certain mystique and reverence about it. Even though it needed a bit of renovation back then, I remember the first time I walked in and looked around – that was the League Cup Final in 1984. You never went to Wembley then, unless your club was in a cup final, that was a massive thing and a memorable moment and occasion, the first all-Merseyside final. Wembley then had a special place in English football which I think has just disappeared now, it's over-exposed.

I'd also say seeing Everton in the Cup Winners' Cup Final in Rotterdam, 1985. European football was different, we weren't cosmopolitan and you were going into new territory – the travelling European fan then had a really different experience. When clubs came here, you knew nothing about them, no satellite TV, no press coverage – maybe something in *World Soccer*. You saw no club football from other countries, only World Cups and European finals, so there was a mystique all round.

# Keith Buxton

Keith was born in 1961 and went to his first game at Portsmouth's Fratton Park in 1975. He has been attending football games at all levels ever since.

***What are your earliest football memories – can you remember a particular game on TV, or a match you went to?***

I never had much interest in football in my early years in the 60s and to my shame I have no memory of England winning the World Cup when I was five. You would have thought the street would have celebrated but nothing springs to mind. I did ask my older brother (ten years older) once and he said it was on but you went out and played with friends.

It all changed for me in 1970 when in junior school my friends were talking about the cup final and how much they wanted Leeds to win it. I decided then to support Chelsea. With it being the first-ever Wembley replay I do remember watching it in the evening. I was upset when the Chelsea goalkeeper was kicked in the knee and could only hobble about. When Leeds scored to go 1-0 up I shouted at my brother that it wasn't fair.

At this point my interest increased, especially as I had agreed to take my brother's bet of 6d on who would win the cup. Our mother decided that it was too late for me to watch the second half as there was school in the morning. At breakfast I was told Leeds had won 2-1 and I handed over my money to big brother. I was informed by friends at school, the next day, of the correct result and got my money back from my brother at tea that evening.

After that I took an interest and watched live football when it was on. I remember very blurry pictures of the 1970 World Cup.

Fast forward to January 1975 and my older brother said he was taking me and our younger brother to our first match. Brian was 25 then, I was about to turn 15 and Chris was 10. We lived in Gosport, Hampshire and our local league team was Portsmouth. It was an exciting time and we entered Fratton Park from Frogmore Road where the black and white Tudor-style buildings are. The opponents were Sunderland who had won the cup in 1973 but were still in Division Two. It is a cliché but true that the first time you see a professional pitch you are struck by how green it is. This might have been exaggerated to me as we had a black and white TV at home and there were no manicured lawns on our council estate.

The game was marvellous. I recognised the Sunderland players from the recent cup final and Jim Montgomery was right in front of us as we stood on the Fratton End terraces. I also learned an important lesson that day, we left before the end to "beat the rush" and Pompey were winning 3-1. As we walked away from the ground a huge cheer went up. "Oh, Pompey have got another," said Brian. As we got back to the car and drove home the radio informed us of the final score: Portsmouth 4 Sunderland 2. I think I have only left a game early two or three times since that day.

### *Who was your favourite team and players growing up?*

Chelsea were my team right from the beginning. I was pleased in school that my house team colours were blue. In games I had Mum sew a white stripe on my shorts just like Chelsea's. Peter Osgood was my favourite, followed by Peter Bonetti. Many years later I was on holiday in Bognor staying at Butlins. Peter Osgood was coaching groups of youngsters but I was too shy to go over and speak to him.

### *What is the most memorable game you have been to?*

There are lots and it is difficult to whittle them down. My first game at Stamford Bridge – 28th October 1978, Chelsea 3-3 Norwich, I went up with my best friend Steve and after the game we went to a Yes concert at Wembley Arena. In May 1980 we had our first away trip following Portsmouth when we went to Northampton and saw them clinch promotion to Division

Three on the last day of the season. Northampton's ground only had three sides as it shared the land with the cricket ground.

My first trip up North was following Portsmouth and their away tie at Liverpool in the League Cup in October 1980. Liverpool won 4-1 but there were around 16,000 Pompey supporters in the 32,000 crowd.

Chelsea beating Manchester City 5-4 in the Full Members Cup Final of 1986. The competition was brought in to fill the void of English teams being banned from Europe. Not all the teams entered and the early rounds were sparsely attended. The Football League refused to authorise any league postponements and the final was held on Sunday 23rd March 1986. Chelsea had played at Southampton the day before and City in the Manchester derby. Ken Bates and Peter Swales, the two chairmen, had underwritten the cost of using Wembley. It was a risk as no terrace tickets were issued before the game and it was pay on the day. Over 67,000 attended and Chelsea had a nervous end to the game as they went from 5-1 up to 5-4 in the last five minutes.

***What were your impressions of attending games before the Premier League era – the atmosphere, the facilities at the stadiums?***

The biggest change in the grounds came after the Taylor Review. Before then the changes from the top division being under the FA and not the League was slow. After Hillsborough, the removal of terracing was the biggest change I have ever seen in the game.

The atmosphere was good on terracing and better at Portsmouth than Chelsea. Portsmouth had some excellent seasons in 1980-1984, going from Division Four to Division Two. As my local club, I knew the people around us and winning seasons tend to keep people happy. Chelsea was a different place in the 80s and suffered from a strong National Front presence. They spent four seasons in Division Two and had some awful performances. They lost 6-0 in Rotherham and were almost relegated to Division Three at one point.

Through the 80s I saw Stamford Bridge go downhill as the club lost money year in and year out. For a couple of years in the 70s an administrator was appointed by the bank and no players were purchased for around three years. Free transfers and youth products were the order of the day. The lowest point came when the freehold of the ground was sold and only regained after a lengthy legal battle. It was only then and with grants available from the government that refurbishments and the conversion to an all-seater stadium could be made. It was completed around 2001. The freehold, pitch, turnstiles and naming rights of Chelsea FC are owned by Chelsea Pitch Owners, of which the supporters are the share owners to prevent such events happening again.

### *Do you still have the same level of interest in the game?*

I do and then some but I have lapsed. When I was married for the first time I only attended 15 games in the 1983/84 and 84/85 seasons. I did drop out completely for several years when children came along and I succumbed to live television. For 2002/03 to 2016/17 only 15 games were attended.

My youngest son Alec, born in 1998, asked if we could attend games together on a regular basis and my bug returned and indeed increased. In three seasons I have attended 162 games, 78 of which are Chelsea consecutive home games. Alec, due to various health problems, now concentrates on our local club Gillingham (I moved to Kent in 1987). I often join him there and I also attend county level (step 5) with Chatham Town and Hollands & Blair.

### *What are the main improvements for spectators since the Premier League started?*

In the early years of the FA Premier League 92/93, Premiership 93/94 to 06/07 and then back to the Premier League 07/08, onwards I did not notice many differences. Looking back though you can see the gradual changes, the biggest being the reduction of 42 games to 38. Television gradually took over. At first it was a novelty to be able to see your team's goals. In the old *Match of the Days* there wasn't any recordings other than the two or three selected games.

With each new contract for broadcasters more TV games were added. This then moved your team's kick-off time and day and we had fewer traditional Saturday afternoons. There were plusses of course and the Stamford Bridge I left in May 2002 is different to the cleaner, fresher, more modern one I returned to in 2017. Then again, the Fulham Broadway underground station and District Line trains have also changed for the better.

Seating has changed the game and the freedom of the terrace to choose your spot and move away from certain individuals has gone. At Stamford Bridge behind each goal the club have given up trying to make supporters sit, your seat is only used before the game and at half-time. The West and East stands are for sitting. Of course we pay for the seats and admission prices have increased. I now have a season ticket again it cost £750, £40 a game for the Premier League. I pay separately for cup games from £10 for Grimsby Town in the League Cup to £55 for Bayern Munich in the Champions League.

The away game cap of £30 is a very good idea and hopefully it will continue for many more seasons

My first season ticket at Chelsea was in the early 80s and cost £30 for the season. I occasionally transferred to the benches in the West Stand at the additional cost of 50p per match.

### *Is there anything you miss about attending games in the 1970s and 80s?*

Paying on the day. If you wanted to go to an away game you just turned up. If you were at the ground half an hour before kick-off you got in. Leave it until 15 minutes before and you were caught up in the rush from the pubs. I do remember not being able to get in to one West Ham v Chelsea match in 1981. I think there were only one or two turnstiles open and it was very congested. I made the decision to go around to the home end where I spent a miserable afternoon applauding the West Ham goals as they crushed Chelsea 4-0. Trevor Brooking was magnificent that day.

I also have memories of diverted games. Three of us went up from Portsmouth on New Year's Day 1986 to see West Ham v Chelsea but we heard on the radio the match was postponed due to overnight frost. One side of the pitch was in the shadow of the stand and remained frozen. We were able to detour to Wimbledon v Portsmouth at Plough Lane where the pitch was playable, no big stands there. Pompey won convincingly and

Micky Channon did his traditional windmill arm celebration as his speculative shot went straight through Dave Beasant.

I used to take a pocket radio to games and use the earpiece to keep updated with other games. They were all played on a Saturday afternoon then. You also struck up conversations with other people as they asked the scores. Now most people are bang up-to-date with their smart phones and are placing in-game bets.

The atmosphere has changed over the years and this has advantages and disadvantages, it was difficult sometimes in the 80s when the opposition were in your end and charged after some unseen signal was given. You got out of the way and left it for the "fighters" to deal with. I remember the League Cup semi-final second leg at Stamford Bridge in 1985. Chelsea were already trailing from the first leg and when Sunderland went 3-1 up people were pouring on the pitch to get it abandoned. The game was stopped and mounted police were used to clear the pitch. It was one of the few games I left early.

# Paul Davis

Paul was born in 1961 and made his debut for Arsenal in 1980. He won every domestic honour in his Arsenal career, including league titles in 1989 and 1991, and the 1994 European Cup Winners' Cup. He currently works at the Football Association as Senior Professional Coach Developer.

***What are your earliest football memories – can you remember a particular game on TV, or a match that you went to?***

My memory's pretty sketchy sometimes when I try to look back on earlier times and playing the game and watching football but there are a couple of moments that do stick out – not necessarily individual games but moments that stick out in my mind. Probably when I was round about the age of 10, 11 – I grew up in the south of London, in a place called Stockwell, the clubs nearest to where I lived were Chelsea, Fulham, Crystal Palace, that side of London but funny enough, I supported Arsenal. That came about by Arsenal winning the '71 FA Cup Final when Charlie George scored that goal. That was when I started following the team, but I used to play football with a friend of mine, we used to play Sunday football and his dad had season tickets at Chelsea and although I didn't know it at the time, Chelsea then were renowned for quite bad hooliganism – I'm talking about mid-70s, so I'd be about 13, 14 years old when I first went to a football game because my parents couldn't afford to take me, and I was probably a bit frightened to go to a game.

So my first experience of football, a professional game to watch, was a Chelsea game with my friend's dad at Stamford Bridge. I don't ever remember feeling frightened or scared but I just remember going to the ground – back then, the stadium had a dog track running round it and the stand was so far away from the pitch that you didn't feel you were close enough to the players, I do remember that, and they had the Shed end at that time, Chelsea, which was renowned for rough fans and the shouting and the chanting but I don't remember really feeling as though I was scared. Those were my first memories of going to football.

My first memories of games on TV was obviously *Match of the Day* and I remember watching West Ham and Clyde Best, because he was a black player, probably the only black player in the league at that time. I could identify with him and I thought, if he can be a footballer, then I can be a footballer as well (I was 13, 14). He was up front for West Ham and he always stuck out for me in terms of watching football, I'd always watch out for him. That's what I wanted to be, after watching it on TV and then having gone to a game at Chelsea – I knew that's what I wanted to be.

### *Were there any other players that inspired you when you were growing up?*

Obviously, Pelé at that time was the world's best player and his name was always mentioned, you'd always look out for somebody like him. Then the first team was the Brazilian team that won that World Cup in 1970 – that would be the first World Cup that I watched. I remember that being amazing, because it was the first colour World Cup, I think before that they would have been black and white – I don't remember 1966, I was only 4 or 5 then. It was in Mexico and I remember all the colours, the ticker-tape and just being fascinated by it, that we could watch the games being beamed back. Brazil won it, and Pelé was outstanding, scoring goals, and an outstanding team – people of my generation still talk about that team as being the best team ever. I recommend anyone that hasn't actually seen any clips of that World Cup to Google those games, because the way Brazil played, the players – Rivelino, Pelé, Jairzinho – they were big inspirations in terms of watching football and trying to emulate what those guys did. As for my favourite team, Arsenal, I don't think I ever went to an Arsenal game until I was about 16, so those were my first real memories of my early days watching football.

## *How did you get into the professional game, where were you spotted – of course there were no academies in those days?*

It was a really interesting situation for me, because I was playing for my school team. I was about 12, 13, and I got picked to play for my district team. My district team was South London, and then you're playing other districts, and I suppose if you're playing at that level, above-average standard, at those sort of games scouts would appear. I was spotted playing for my district over in Belair Park, South London – after the game, when I was 13, a guy came up and said he was from Arsenal. He was a scout, are my parents around, would I like to come down to Arsenal? Wow! This was mad, my parents were not around, but I'm going to come down. They did it the right way, they had to speak to my parents – when I told my mum, she wasn't overly keen but I said 'mum, look, this is what I want to do, this is where I want to go.' She wasn't sure, I had to persuade her. In the end, she signed the papers that allowed me to go down and start training at Arsenal, so that's how it all came about.

I started training from the age of 13, two nights a week after school. I used to go down to Arsenal from where we lived, in Stockwell, so it was a bit of a trek and I had to go and make that journey on my own, so I'd finish school and we used to go down. I'd rush home from school, change out of my school clothes into my training gear, got on the Tube, went down to Arsenal, and that was every Tuesday and Thursday for two years I did that. I trained at Arsenal two nights a week and really enjoyed it, made sure I was there on time, did whatever the coach wanted me to do – my mind was just set on being a footballer. I was lucky, a lot of hard work, dedication as well, for the club to say 'we like the look of you,' and they signed me on at 15, 16, so that's when I realised I'd got an opportunity here with this team. Arsenal back then had a real reputation for bringing through younger players – not like now. It's harder now to get through, but they had people like Pat Rice in the team, when I was 14, 15 I had people like Charlie George, Liam Brady and many others who had come through the youth system and you felt, as a young player, that you had an opportunity if you were good enough. That was a real opportunity for me and I just felt I'm not going to let this go and took it with both hands. So it started from there, I got my apprenticeship at 16 – the apprenticeships they don't do now, or they call them different things now, but the apprentices back in those days had to clean the boots, the changing rooms, you had to make sure the stadium was clean, so part of our day was going back to the stadium to make sure everything was looked after. So there were some good life lessons being learnt in there as well as the football – great memories, looking back.

***You made your debut against Spurs at White Hart Lane – what do you remember about that day?***

Yeah, that was amazing, because at the time I didn't realise I was going to play – it was 1979/80, so how that came about was the regular first-team players were in the semi-final of the FA Cup and the semi-final of the European Cup Winners' Cup, so they had these important games coming up and the manager, Terry Neill, didn't want them playing this game against Spurs. There was nothing in the game against Spurs, we couldn't win the title, so the manager decided to put in a few of us youngsters. I was one, Paul Vaessen was another I remember, maybe four of us that were selected to play, and it was an amazing thing because first of all it was against Spurs, and then we won the game 2-1. I didn't know I was playing until maybe two hours before the game, the team was announced – I was in the squad, and then we had a team meeting before the game, and I was playing. A surreal moment really, because that's what I had been dreaming of since I was 10, 11, so seven years later I'm living my dream and then to beat our rivals at their own ground as well put a little bit of added spice to it for me. I don't remember too much of the game, I just remember running out on the pitch and feeling this is quite something – and the fans, we're talking about the old Spurs ground, White Hart Lane, which is a lot tighter than the new stadium, so that was magnified a bit more, the pressure and the excitement of the game, which you can't really describe, but the feeling of having won the game 2-1 was fantastic.

***I grew up watching players like Viv Anderson, Cyrille Regis and Garth Crooks, and I think Brendan Batson had been at Arsenal in the early 70s, but you were the***

***only black player in the team at that time — did you feel like a trail-blazer; what were your early experiences in the Football League?***

That's an interesting one, because I look back on that now and think, wow, that was something then. At the time, I didn't realise the enormity of the situation but now I really do. I often look back and I think that was something, and the reason I'm able to do that is because people stop me in the street, particularly people from Afro-Caribbean backgrounds, and say 'back then, you were so much to us,' and it's not just one or two, it's quite a lot of people in recent years who say, 'we watched you, we could identify with you, we watched Arsenal because you were there.' At the time, you're just playing the game, trying to get ahead in the business, it's only in recent years that I've really come to recognise the impact of the fact that I was playing for Arsenal at that time has had on so many people. Even now, they still remember it, so it's such a huge thing for me to feel as if I've had an effect on all football people really, but particularly people from Afro-Caribbean backgrounds and people of colour who at that time didn't feel comfortable, didn't feel welcome – I know that from my mum, who wouldn't go to games for fear of violence and trouble, of being made to feel unwelcome. I know what it was like, even though looking back, I was in a bubble in terms of being at Arsenal. I was protected in a sense, but I was getting abused from the stands by opposition supporters so it wasn't total isolation but I think I was treated a little bit differently because I was at Arsenal, than if I'd worked in a shop or something like that. It's quite a big thing in the black community that they were able to have somebody like me at such a big club as Arsenal.

It's a good question because Brendan Batson was before me, and I think he played a handful of games, six or seven, and I did keep a tab on what players of a black background had done, and followed their career. I did see Brendan a couple of weeks ago and we spoke briefly about those times – he went on and played at West Brom, and I followed his career, and Luther Blissett, Laurie Cunningham, Cyrille Regis, Garth Crooks, all a little bit older than me but they were all players that I could hang onto their tails, and think 'if they did, I can do it.' The difficulties were there, definitely, going away and trying to play at away games, you had to be really mentally strong to make sure you stayed on your job and nothing distracted you – it was tough, but I think when you're driven, you can put all those things to one side.

***You had a lot of success in your career – league titles and cup wins – was there a particular moment, could you pick a highlight of your career?***

Obviously, my debut would always be one of the biggest highlights, and winning the trophies we did is always going to stick in my mind but I think the biggest one, that I didn't actually play in, that will always live long in the memory, is '89. An amazing situation – for those people that don't know, it was a season that went to the last game, down to these two teams to win the league and it's Arsenal v Liverpool. At Liverpool, and they've got a really good team, people like John Barnes and John Aldridge and some really outstanding players, and we needed to win by two clear goals to win the title, nobody gave us a chance – and we went up there and did it! I was injured but it was such an iconic game and moment, to win the title in the last game, and the way we won it, with the last kick of the game, that's got to stick out. I didn't play in that game, but I would have done if I was fit, so it's got so many connotations for me, so happy to be part of the team, that squad, but not actually to be in the team on that night, that wins it, it's such a disappointment. I'd definitely have to say that night was a stand-out.

Then playing in all the finals, so the FA Cup Final against Sheffield Wednesday, the League Cup and we won that, and then the European Cup Winners' Cup – one of the biggest disappointments was being out of Europe when English teams were banned – looking back now, that was such a big blow. At the time, OK you're banned, not able to play in European football, you just get on with it, but after your career's ended, you think of the five years we were banned and what we could have done as players and clubs, and around that time Arsenal were doing pretty well so we would have been in Europe if we were able to take part. You have some regrets, but things happen and there's not much you can do about it – English fans were pretty bad when they travelled abroad, and UEFA felt that they had to make a stand on English clubs, and that lasted five years.

***You played against all the famous midfielders in the First Division over your career – who were your most difficult opponents, or the best players you played against?***

I always say, without a question of a doubt, the hardest player I played against was Glenn Hoddle. He was just the most gifted player I'd ever come up against. We played directly opposite each other, I'd be asked to mark him – I don't know whether his manager told him to mark me! He would definitely more often than not try to run the game – the thing about Glenn, he had two fantastic feet – left foot, right foot just the same, equally as good both sides, his vision was incredible, he could not only see it, but deliver it as well. His feel for the game, as I get older I just appreciate it even more, there's not many people that I've seen who could play football like him, so Glenn Hoddle without a doubt. He could score, he could create – he wasn't a defensive player but for what he could do going that way, you could forego what he couldn't do – attacking-wise. I've seen him do things on the pitch that I thought, 'wow, this guy's something else.' I always felt going into the game playing against him was going to be a test, always made sure that I was concentrating, that I didn't dive in, stayed on my feet, because I knew if there was one second, he'd be off, he'd be gone, he'd score or create something – so definitely Glenn.

Other players were people like Graeme Souness and Bryan Robson, big big players of the time – late 70s, 80s – and again they were different types of players. Bryan Robson was different to Glenn, but could be as effective in a different way – he was more up and down midfield, very strong in the tackle, could score goals, could create goals. I always felt a little bit more at ease with marking or playing against Bryan Robson as opposed to Glenn, that he was more 'readable' and that I could probably predict what he was going to try and do. Then Graeme Souness was a tough, tough player – he didn't mess around, he got his tackles in but he could play as well, so there was all different types of players, but those three were at the top of their game in a similar position to me and you always knew you had a game on with those three.

Then later on, people like Paul Scholes and one or two others – of course Paul Gascoigne, I played against him quite a few times, he was a tough guy, strong, always got his body in there, could shield the ball well. Loved his football, even though we were professional players on the pitch he was like a kid, an exuberant kid just doing things that you would do in the playground. I played against some really decent players – and against Parma, [Gianfranco] Zola in his early days, he could only be about 20, 21, and coming up against him I remember thinking 'this guy's going to be a player' so I've been fortunate enough to play against some really outstanding players. International-wise, I was in the England squads but I didn't actually play for England on the international stage but I played against a lot of players in club football that were internationals. Steve McMahon at Liverpool, [Neil] Webb at Nottingham Forest and then he went to Man United, [Steve] Hodge at Spurs, there were other guys that were difficult to play against but the three that I mentioned, they were the stand-out players.

Then you've got to bring into the discussion the pitches in those days, so different to what they are now. My local team is Barnet, I went to their game at the weekend and one of the directors was showing me the pitch and saying how bad it was, and I said, 'if you think that's bad!' I'm looking at it and it's really flat – it wasn't all grass because there's too many games been played on it but it's flat and there weren't too many bumps. It's such a big change from back in the day when I started out to what it is now – the game has changed.

***I think Highbury was generally in decent condition, but the Baseball Ground at Derby was notorious, Old Trafford was pretty bad – what was it like playing on the mud-baths, especially as a ball-playing midfielder?***

Looking back now, I think we did well as professional footballers to produce some of the football that we did, because some of the pitches were really terrible. The ones that you've mentioned, the Baseball Ground was particularly bad – at Arsenal we had a decent pitch, we had an oval bit in the middle that wasn't totally flat, where the centre-circle was, it was a bit of a dome in the middle of the pitch. I always felt, why can't they just flatten the pitch off, but as for condition, it was one of the better pitches in the league. I always felt Everton had a nice pitch at the time but back then, if there was heavy rain then the pitches just got cut up and they just played, they didn't cancel games. The grass now is different, they've got fibres and plastic in it but then it was just natural grass that would get dug up if you did a slide – these guys now that do a knee-slide, if you did that back then it'd ruin the pitch! In those days we played in so many treacherous conditions, mud-baths particularly in the middle of the pitch – the sides often didn't seem to get so bad, penalty areas got really bad. Yeah, pitches have changed!

**The alternative to the mud-baths were the plastic pitches – at QPR and Luton – how was it playing on them?**

We found it really tough playing on those, 'cause it was their first introduction, we played on the first plastic pitches, we didn't know what to expect. Obviously the home team had a good advantage, they were used to it – we used to play at Luton, QPR, I think Preston North End had one, I remember playing at Oldham when they were up in the Premier League. I never liked them, always felt uncomfortable and it wasn't great on the joints because you were just pounding and twisting on hard ground, and the ball would skid off if it had been raining, you had to make sure you had the right footwear. It was quite hard to get the right balance between how the ball was going to spin off the astroturf, and making sure of your footing – we always tried to prepare well but we never played our best football on those sort of pitches. I was glad when they reverted back to grass, real pitches.

**I wanted to ask about tackling – from a fan's point of view, it seems like we've gone from one extreme, where players didn't really get enough protection, to the other, where free-kicks are given for virtually any physical contact. What's your perspective on that?**

I'm a little bit frustrated in terms of that, because I feel as though it's a physical game and that's being taken out of it a little bit. I get the idea that you've got to look after each other, protect your opponent, that goes without saying, but it's a fine balance between taking that side of the game away and looking after professionals. When I first played tackling from behind was allowed, you could go through people, you used to talk about it, 'just go in behind him, he won't want the ball after that' so that's been taken away, fair enough you don't want anyone getting badly injured but back then people used to be reckless and get away with it, so I get the idea. But then you see some of these silly fouls, where he's not really touched him, and the ref's blown up and stopped it. I understand that things move forward, but I do feel the loss of some of the physicality of the game. We've gained in other ways, it's become quicker, more skilful – so it does change.

*A lot of the more technical midfielders from your era went on to play abroad – Liam Brady at the start of the 80s, then Ray Wilkins and Gordon Cowans in Italy, Glenn Hoddle and Ricky Hill to France later on. Were you ever tempted to play abroad – was there a league you would have liked to play in?*

There was talk towards the end of the 80s, talk of Paris St-Germain – it was all in the papers. It was a time when I wasn't getting games at Arsenal and I felt 'well, I want to play' and I went to the club and I said, 'cause I'm not playing, can I leave,' and they said no. George Graham was the manager – another big thing, the Bosman rule wasn't in then, so if the club said no you can't go anywhere, that was it, end of story. There was no Twitter, you couldn't put out your story, the clubs always had control over what went out – a lot of propaganda goes out from clubs to make sure that fans are onside and the players didn't really have a lot of power, so that's been a massive change in the game. For me, that was a moment that could have been different, the club saying yes and then maybe I would have gone, but no, it never got to that stage.

My style was definitely more suited to that continental way of playing. I liked passing – short and long passes – trying to control a game through the tempo and I could look after myself, I could make tackles. The English game wasn't really around that, it was around fights, tackles and physicality, and my game wasn't naturally that, I had to find those skills to be able to survive. I always look back on my style, and talking about Glenn again, to me Glenn Hoddle should have won 150 England caps, he played about 50 times, it was just the time – his style wasn't suited to the First Division at that time – he would probably be more suited to today's game, so to do what he did in those times was just unreal.

***Finally, could you say a little about your current role in football, and how that relates to some of the changes that you've maybe seen between your playing days and now?***

My role now is Senior Professional Coach Developer, so I'm involved in a lot of the Pro Licence courses that we do here at the FA [St George's Park], then I do 'A' Licence as well. I support some of our more senior coaches through those qualifications, and I really enjoy it, the study and the learning off people. I enjoy studying the game, watching the game, seeing the changes that are going on, good and bad, so it keeps me involved in the game. I enjoy watching people work and then having conversations with them about what they're doing, why they're doing it, just helping people develop their coaching skills and leadership skills. Yeah, the game has changed tremendously and it's continuing to change – there's been so many changes it's hard to put it in a nutshell – the money, the TV money has made amazing changes, the movement of people. So back when I started, it was just British players that I was up against, I remember the first player that was in the Arsenal team was a guy called Vladimir Petrović, he was the only foreign player in our squad back then and there were probably only a few in the whole division. So that change, the pitches, there's been so many changes in football.

# Ron Futcher

Ron was born in 1956 in Chester, and spent the first part of his career at his home-town club before moves to Luton Town and Manchester City, both alongside his twin brother Paul. He played for several seasons in the North American Soccer League, where he became the fourth-highest all-time goalscorer in the league. After returning to England in 1984, he represented a further six Football League teams. He now lives in Florida, where he has coached at a number of clubs.

*What are your earliest football memories?*

Obviously for me, being brought up in a big family and with a twin, me and him like most kids then in that era spent 8-10 hours a day kicking a ball outside. My dad used to drive a big wagon with Shell and my mum was looking after nine kids, so on a Saturday if possible they used to go to the British Legion at 7:30pm. My older brothers and sisters were generally out of the house so me and our kid used to know *Match of the Day* was coming on at 10 o'clock, we'd close the curtains so it was pitch black, sit down with a packet of crisps and just couldn't wait for the game to start and watch it. We just used to think, 'look at this!' That started at five or six, onwards we got more into it, sitting on the sofa saying 'one day this could be us' – we were living the dream through the TV at that early stage.

My dad used to take us when he could, when he could afford it, to Old Trafford so we grew up supporting Manchester United, watching Denis Law, George Best, Bobby Charlton, all that era. So that was another massive nugget, for us to get there and play at Old Trafford, play at those sorts of places. We'd go and smell the atmosphere, imagine what it would be like to be there one day.

## *Were there any players that you particularly admired, growing up?*

Even at an early age, I was always playing up front and our Paul was generally playing in midfield. I used to love Denis Law, the way he celebrated lifting his arm up, holding his cuff – I thought that was brilliant. He just had this quality, arrogance, he was a finisher, so for me, Denis Law.

## *What was your route into professional football at Chester?*

To cut a long story short, back in the day of course there were no academies at clubs, so generally you had to play on your county team – for me and Paul it was Cheshire schoolboys. We managed to get on that team a year early, under-15s, so we'd play against Lancashire boys – which is now divided into different areas but back then was all of Lancashire, so it was a really, really tough team. Nearly every player was affiliated to a big club, but me and our kid were affiliated to Chester. I remember our manager saying to us that England Schoolboys were having a get-together at Lancaster University in a couple of weeks and they want you and Paul to be part of the group. We went and did a registration, and all the players' names were read out, and it was David, Everton, so-and-so, Liverpool, Manchester United... Ron Futcher, Chester! They were 92nd in the league and it was quite comical, but ironically enough, none of those other players went on to make it, only Paul and I did.

So Cheshire schoolboys was a passport for us to get to Chester, we signed associated schoolboys forms there. We could have gone to Wolves or other clubs in Division One, but we wanted to stay local with our home-town team, and we actually thought if we stayed at Chester, we'd probably have a quicker opportunity to get in the first team, get spotted and move on. And that's what happened – we got into the first team at 16, by 17 – on our 17th birthday – we signed a pro contract, and three months later we went to Luton, so it worked out exactly how we planned it.

### *When did you make your debut, and what do you remember of the game?*

It was against Workington away [October 1973]. I was 16 and Paul was already in the team, so I remember the local paper taking a picture of us with our boots tied round our neck, getting on to the team bus. It was a really low-key event, there wasn't many there [862], cold midweek night at Workington – that was it! I think I played six or seven more games, then Paul went and I went, so we weren't really in the first team for very long.

For us the motivation at Chester was, we were apprentices – we didn't train much because we only had a group of about 18-20 pros. We trained with them but we had to spend most of our time cleaning the stands, picking the mud up off the pitch after the groundsman rolled it, so we used to train ourselves between 12 and 1 o'clock. We'd finish training and come into the boot room, there'd be 20 pairs of dirty, filthy boots we had to get ready for training the next day. It was a slog for two years, cleaning and working. If it wasn't for us doing our own training at lunchtimes and tea-breaks, we wouldn't have got much training – but that's how it was, you just got on with it, that was an apprenticeship.

### *What was it like as a centre-forward in the Football League in that era – I imagine it was pretty physical?*

From an early age you have to look after yourself because starting in the reserves at 15, you're playing against established pros, generally older, who were never quite going to make it higher than the level they were at. We've got these two blond-haired kids, a centre-forward going past these defenders – if they don't win the ball, believe me, you're not going past them! There was no mercy, the refereeing wasn't the greatest, the pitches were heavy, muddy, so they could slide in from six feet away and take you out. You just got on with it, get up and shake yourself down and think next time you'll make sure you don't get caught. You learn how to manage your game at an early age – you knew if the ball comes long, kicked by the keeper, a big centre-half is going to come in and take you out. You just braced yourself!

***You moved from Luton to Minnesota [to the North American Soccer League in 1976], on loan initially – how did that come about?***

At some stage before the end of the season, Freddie Goodwin, the ex-Birmingham manager who was now the coach at Minnesota Kicks, a team which had just been established that year, was looking for players. They came and did a presentation, because Freddie knew Harry Haslam, who said there might be a few players interested at Luton – Jimmy Husband, Alan West, Adrian Alston, Jimmy Ryan – so he said, come and show the video, then any players who are interested can speak up. They put this video on, and it was fantastic! Flying into America, you get an apartment, brand-new Camero, four months playing in these stadiums, double the money you're earning at Luton – you're thinking, 'it's a no-brainer.' I thought I wasn't going to get a sniff, all the senior pros would snap it up, but they were looking for a centre-forward, a midfielder and a couple of defenders. None of the strikers put their hand up, so I said, 'I'm here, I'll come across' – I was only 18, nearly 19. So Freddie jumped on it, with me, Alan West and Steve Litt, there was three of us, and that's how it evolved. I went over and it was fantastic. It was a brand-new franchise, the owners were a couple of guys who owned big supermarkets, with plenty of money and they brought in Freddie and Roy McCrohan, who had been coaching at Luton.

***How was that experience, playing there in that first season?***

I was only 18-19, and when I got there Alan Willey, a Geordie lad from Middlesbrough, was already there and instantly I was playing up front with him, we were the same age. We had some good players, Geoff Barnett in goal, Ron Webster from Derby the right-back, Frank Spraggon from Middlesbrough the left-back, Stevie Litt, Alan Merrick from West Brom – that was the back four. Alan West, who was a great player from Luton, we had a guy called Patrick 'Ace' Ntsoelengoe, unbelievable player, me and Alan Willey up front. It was fantastic, we were getting 20-30,000, you'd come onto the pitch, they'd shout your name and you'd run into the centre circle, all these cheerleaders, you'd line up and feel really important. You were playing against Pelé, Beckenbauer, Neeskens, Cruyff, Best, getting good money, flying to L.A., Chicago, San Francisco, Hawaii – this is ridiculous! We actually got to the Soccer Bowl [NASL Final] that year, we should have won it, beat 3-0 by Toronto, Eusébio scored. We got measured up for these rings, I've still got mine [from winning with Tulsa in 1983], and it was a fantastic experience.

*After Luton, you made the move to Manchester City, where Paul had already gone. Did you notice a step up in terms of play and facilities?*

It wasn't always recognised at Luton that we got in the team early, Harry Haslam threw us in the team very young, you don't get that incubation period, a few months to settle in, play one game in three. For us it was, 'in you go,' you have to score goals, you have to keep them out at the back – and by the way, you're on your own, not getting a lot of help. You're playing against Norman Hunter, Ron Harris, top internationals on heavy pitches at Luton, and we did play Manchester City a few times and both got really good reviews. I'm assuming that's why they came in for Paul and later on they came in for me.

I remember I was in America at the time, and David Pleat was manager at Luton. He wanted to change things around, and me and Paul never really got on with him, he just wasn't our cup of tea. When he became manager he clearly wanted to get rid of some players – I don't know why he wanted to get rid of us playing-wise, because we were young, in the team and doing well. So he moved Paul out to City and I was in America for four months, Pleaty called me up and said, 'We're selling you to Blackpool' – he wanted to sign Bob Hatton – and I just said, 'I'm not going to Blackpool!' I wasn't going to drop a division, if anything I was either staying or moving up a division. At 6 o'clock the next morning I got a call from Tony Book at Man City, and he said we're going to sign you, we've agreed a fee with Luton. I flew back, went to Man City, the Chairman was [Peter] Swales, walked into his office – there were no agents, you had to do your own deal, in fact they told you what you were going to get and you either took it or you didn't. Tony Book was there, and I said there's just one thing – I haven't got a car, I've just come from the States, can you get me a car for at least three-four weeks until I buy one, and they said, 'We can do that.'

So I played on Tuesday for the reserves, Nottingham Forest away, we had a Scottish coach who's passed on now, Dave Ewing was his name – he was ruthless. We're playing at Forest, winning 3-0, I've scored two in the first half, thinking this is great, come in at half-time and he waded into me, gave me the biggest bollocking I've ever had in my career. I'm thinking, am I missing something here? I've just come off the plane, signed for Man City, I've scored twice, and he's telling me 'you're lazy, you're not chasing back, not doing this…' I said something like 'what are you talking about?' and he brought me off! I thought then, this is a different level, this is going to be tough, it's a big step up here.

I was training, I didn't get near a sniff of the first team, didn't get a lot of help from senior players, Brian Kidd was great, Mick Channon wasn't. Dave Watson, Willie Donachie who I knew anyway, Peter Barnes, Gary Owen – some of the younger players were good, because they were our age, but the older players didn't really help too much because they didn't want to lose their places. Channon was playing for England, Kiddo, Barnesy, so it was going to be tough for me to get in. Our kid had just about got in the team, playing alongside Dave Watson, but he found it tough. Where he was used to taking responsibility at Luton, organising, pinging balls which he could do all day long, Dave Watson would do that at City – and he was playing for England, of course Paul would give him the ball. So that hindered his game, and I was playing in the reserves, scoring goals, and eventually they put me in and I scored, a hat-trick at Chelsea, and the week after against Tottenham, we won 2-0 and I scored. The next week, it was Manchester United away at Old Trafford, and don't forget in those days there was only one sub, so the team sheet went up on the Friday for Saturday's game, I'm in the reserves and Roger Palmer was the sub. I'd just scored four in two games and was bombed out! No explanation, get on with it, back in the reserves.

I was sub a few times, but all the time I was at City it never really felt like I was part of the club. I think it was the expectation maybe, but I was never given too much of a chance, even though I played 14 games and scored 7, never really got that extended opportunity. You had Kidd, Channon – established internationals, so it was always going to be tough. When Book was sacked, Malcolm Allison came in, and there was an instant dislike toward certain players, and unfortunately me and Paul were in that group – he wasn't very nice.

***Did that influence your decision to stay in the States permanently [with Minnesota], instead of only summers on loan, as you'd done previously?***

Yeah, they just came in out of the blue with a three-year contract, I was still only 23, it was good money – for that time, it was unbelievable money – but more importantly, it was the fact that I enjoyed it over there anyway. I knew the people at Minnesota, it was a great place to live and to play, so given that I was unhappy at Man City, it was a no-brainer really. I said yes straight away and that was it.

***You had a couple more moves in the States, won a Soccer Bowl in '83 with Tulsa – what do think happened for that league to go from being quite successful, to going out of business in a short space of time?***

I don't know how it true it was, but I did hear at the time that owning a sports franchise for five years was almost like a tax-free write-off for these businesses. After five years we [Minnesota] were gone, and at some points we were averaging over 30,000 – against the bigger teams, we'd get 50,000. We were a good role model for other clubs, we had tail-gating, people there early, great support, good media coverage and a successful team. But we started bringing in Charlie George, Trevor Francis, people like that, and they're not coming for the money we're earning – more like ten times that – and that's what teams started doing. We played the Los Angeles Aztecs, Bestie's team, in a stadium with a 100,000 capacity [the Coliseum], and there was 3,000 there. Then we flew to Hawaii, stayed four days, fantastic, and played in front of another 3,000 people. It's not going to work, is it? We went to Tampa Bay, where I live now, and they had a great thing going, getting 25-

30,000, but then they started doing the same thing, paying exorbitant money for players and then the crowds started diminishing. That was the start of the end, unfortunately.

**When you did come back to Europe, you went to Holland – how did that come about?**

After Tulsa, through Wim Suurbier, the Dutch international who recently passed away, fantastic guy, he was a coach, I loved playing for him – way ahead of his time in terms of his coaching, the way he talked to players, pre-match meals, everything. Tulsa was on its way out and the league was in trouble, though I had a good season we got beaten in the play-offs and I thought 'here I go again, another situation where I'll be looking for a club.' Anyway, Wim rang me and asked how I felt about coming to Holland, said he knew the coach at NAC Breda who spoke good English, and said 'why don't you come over? We'll meet you at Schipol airport, take you to a hotel, see if we can do a deal.' So I went over with my wife, we were in a big car with the owner, and he asked me, 'Ron, what are your strengths?' I went, 'If you're looking for somebody to run in behind, I ain't going to do it, but if you want someone to hold the ball up, get on the end of crosses, depending on how you play, that's my strength.'

OK, so we did the deal, they gave me a house, a car, decent money, and an option that if any club comes in for me, I can get 25% of the signing-on fee or any profit. But they were in hard times, they were a great set of lads, but they only trained twice a week. So I'm stuck in Holland, two kids going to a school where they don't speak English, we're training twice a week and I'm bored. We were playing in a small stadium, which was great, because it's packed out – the first two games were PSV Eindhoven away, and Ajax at home. PSV we lost 4-1, scored there, then we got beaten 2-0 by Ajax, they've got Rijkaard and all those internationals playing, played the next ten games and scored six or seven goals, a hat-trick in the Dutch FA Cup. I was still getting slated because the team was struggling, I was getting frustrated, we're playing on Sunday tea-times, playing with a sweeper dropping on the six-yard box, it was boring and my kids weren't happy there. So I called our kid up at Barnsley, I heard they were looking for a striker, he had a word with

Bobby Collins the manager, and I got a phone call. He asked how much I wanted a week, and I said, 'I'll have whatever our kid's earning.' I went to the owner at Breda, and he said I'd have to forfeit my 25% of the transfer fee so I said 'fine, it's not going to be much anyway' – they did the deal and I went to Barnsley.

***When you returned to England in 1984, did you notice any change in the English game?***

I think it was more or less the same, grounds hadn't changed, same mentality, one sub, shared the same bath – the good old times, same world.

***Your next move was to Oldham, where you played against Paul for the first time. How did you find that?***

It was quite awkward, Paul was playing at the back for Barnsley – I didn't play against him many times. I knew exactly how he played, he knew exactly how I played, it just didn't feel right. What he was really, really good at was seeing the danger before it happened, so if the ball was coming in to strikers, nine times out of ten he'd see the pass and nip in, and make you look a bit of a clown. He could read the game so well, that was always in my mind. I didn't enjoy playing against him for that reason, because we were so close. It was a good thing it didn't work out as too many times.

***You still had a few good seasons left, at Bradford, Port Vale, Burnley...***

It was funny because at Oldham and Bradford I had to play my position – by that I mean I didn't have people running off me, I had to hold it up, win headers, come back and mark the centre-half, lead the line and score goals. All that for £350-400 quid! When I went to Port Vale it was different because I had Robbie Earle bombing past me, I had Darren Beckford, I played a bit deeper but I still scored goals, we were good off set-pieces. When I went to Crewe, we had Craig Hignett, loads of young players and Burnley was the same, with Roger Eli and John Francis. It was a different role, and a role I enjoyed – Roger Eli used to take all the knocks, take the defenders away so I could just turn in the hole and knock balls in behind. It was a different ending to my career but I still managed to get a few goals. They were good teams, at Bradford, at Vale.

## *What were your most memorable experiences over the course of your career?*

One of my most enjoyable periods was that four summers in Minnesota. The pressure wasn't there, I could enjoy it without the expectation of having to score 20 goals. You didn't have promotion or relegation, just play-offs, and if you didn't make them, you had next season, not going up or down a level. There was the weather, everything, but in terms of the actual intensity I enjoyed Luton because me and Paul got in the team together, we got in the first team early, you had the buzz.

I remember at half past twelve on a Friday when they put the team sheet up with a safety pin, you had 30 players sitting in the changing room waiting, everybody would run up. Then finding out you're playing, against Arsenal, or Liverpool, they'd tell you to be at the ground 10 o'clock the next morning, we'd go pre-match to a hotel at Harpenden. I used to love going there, but the best thing was coming back, half past one on the coach, through the centre of Luton – you could smell the atmosphere of a game day, the roads were packed with supporters. Sitting on the coach, the adrenalin was unbelievable. Then you get to the stadium, you could already hear the noise when you go into the tunnel, onto the pitch at 2 o'clock, looking around at the supporters – take a deep breath. That was almost better than the game, sometimes the match could be a bit flat or whatever, the build-up was fantastic.

Then obviously, playing at Old Trafford, Liverpool, Tottenham, Chelsea, Newcastle, thinking 'I can't believe I'm here' – and you're playing! So I think the time at Luton, experiencing that for the first time, and the most enjoyable time was in America, where there was no pressure. Then the most rewarding time was probably towards the end, when you're helping young players at the beginning of their careers, at Crewe and Port Vale. They're actually listening, and you feel a sense of obligation in the changing room, to calm them down, give them a bit of advice – I got a lot of gratification by doing that. They were young players who really wanted to do well, and they liked me because they could see I wasn't there just for a pay-off, they could see I was giving 100% when I was playing, chasing back and not walking around, not that big-timer in the changing room. On the training ground, helping with finishing, timing your run, things like that. It was just a fantastic 15-20 years – most people see it, but they never live it.

## *Who were your most difficult opponents among centre-halves?*

I think if you're playing in the same division, you're going to come across the same centre-halves at different times, whereas in the First Division, I wasn't there that long. I did play against Hansen and Lawrenson a few times, and didn't see the ball for 90 minutes – that wasn't just them necessarily, that was the team. There was Shotton and Briggs, at Oxford, Mal [Shotton] I got to know when he was at Barnsley with our kid, he wasn't actually that dirty, he was just hard, he'd hit you with everything. Now Gary Briggs, when he tackled you he'd purposely run his studs down the back of your calves, all the time – some centre-halves, you could almost say 'hey, what are you doing?, but not with him, he'd just get you again and again.

Allan Evans at Villa, a couple from West Brom who were really hard, one was Wile, and there were about half a dozen you knew what you were getting – 90% of the time fair – that's just how it was in those days. Nobody complained, you just got on with it. I could look after myself, I wasn't frightened of them, it was just more that you knew what was coming from them!

## *Who were the best players that you played with and against?*

One of the best players I played with was my brother, I thought he was a great player and that's being biased I know, but he actually was. The reason I say that is, I played with a lot of centre-halves who could defend but couldn't pass the ball, but he could do that – and pass the ball specifically to me, which helps! I thought he was very under-rated, and it didn't help him going to City, it hindered him. Asa Hartford was a top player at Man City, great attitude, leader, give you everything, and he would give you encouragement, one of the few players to do that. There's been so many good players – at Man City, we had Peter Barnes on the wing, he had a natural talent.

Neeskens, Cruyff – we played Washington at home, Cruyff was playing and I scored four that day. I'm not mentioning it because of that, but in the paper the next day he said 'we didn't deserve anything from the game, and I just want to say well done to the No. 18 on their team, the boy Futcher, he was tremendous' – I've still got that! He's another player who just oozed quality when he got the ball, his touch... 'Ace' Ntsoelengoe, he was unbelievable, as good as any European player in terms of technical ability, with the ball at his feet, change of pace, scoring goals – he had everything. Played against Gordon Banks, scored against him, there were a lot of top players in the North American Soccer League.

*You didn't have an agent, but how did transfer negotiations work?*

In the 80s especially, I think what it was that you went through the PFA if you needed a bit of guidance. My mate Mick McGuire, he worked for the PFA under Gordon Taylor, and I used to call Mick up and say 'look, I'm going to so-and-so,' and he could find out what the best players were earning through his contacts. You had a bit of guidance but that was it, never had an agent. I guess you didn't really need one because clubs didn't negotiate with you.

*I wanted to ask about some of the changes since the Premier League:*

*1 Physical contact – it seems to have gone from one extreme, where there was not enough protection for the more skilful players especially, to the other, where tackling has virtually gone out of the game. What's your take on that?*

When I played, in that era, it was just how it was, and everybody accepted it as part of the game. It was the culture of the game, and nobody complained too much – now that's changed and I guess with the foreign players initiating it, any kind of contact and they go down. The referees have changed with it, now if they see contact, more times than not they give a free-kick. With the speed of the game now, the pitches being so much better, the ball moving quicker, any kind of contact they go down.

The way the game's played, it's not so much into the centre-forward and playing off him, the game was designed in that kind of mould, it's so fast, players are moving so quickly, fitness levels are so much better, in terms of diet, nutrition. Don't forget back when I played, you didn't have to do a warm-up, so you could get to the ground at 2 o'clock, sit and read the programme until half two, put your gear on and go out. Can you imagine that now? I remember times at Manchester City, being in the changing room at quarter to three, Micky Channon would come in with his kit on and say 'sorry I'm late, I've been watching the horse racing in the bar' – then he'd go out and play! Now they're paying someone a hundred grand just to take the players' warm-up. If I was playing in this era now, I think I would have played longer because I would have been fitter, more supple, and I would have had a better range to my game because the coaching, the ideas, have improved. The protection for players is better.

Young players have got a fantastic opportunity, in terms of how the game's evolved in terms of technical ability and fitness levels, but where they miss out is in the opportunity to play, because of all the foreigners. You're paying all this money out, and you've got to play them.

***2 Pitches – you've mentioned the state of them looking back, compared to perfect surfaces now. How did you feel about the plastic pitches in the NASL and at Oldham?***

Roger Eli [ex-Burnley] sent me this clip the other day, of me playing against Newcastle for Luton, and from one penalty area to the other, the pitch is just covered in sand! So when I was at Oldham and they got the astroturf, I absolutely loved it. I'd played on it in a lot of games in America, and when Oldham got it, although it wasn't the best, it was great for strikers. When the ball comes into you, defenders can't slide in and take you out – they just can't do it, so I loved it. People like Micky Quinn didn't like it, he was heavy-framed, his touch wasn't great anyway but one of my strengths was my touch, and the ball was always coming in nicely, on the floor especially.

Back in the day the training grounds were crap anyway, and the pitches by November were crap, so you just got used to playing on those pitches and set your game up. I remember my legs used to get heavy quite early in games, and now I know why. Over here [in Florida] I've been coaching for 14 years, and the pitches are unbelievable, like Wembley, and these are for 11-12-year-old kids – they don't know they're born! Training facilities have definitely helped improve kids technically.

### 3 The grounds themselves – a lot of clubs have moved to new grounds, they're all-seater. How conscious were you as a player of the noise from the terraces and the atmosphere in the ground?

You're definitely aware of it, especially at Luton where the ground was quite tight anyway, and back in the day you'd get 12-15,000 (the capacity was 18,000) pretty close to the pitch. Especially in the 70s and 80s when there was a lot of crowd trouble, the opposing fans trying to get into the home end, you'd have a corner and suddenly all hell would break loose behind the pitch, so you were definitely aware of it. Even when I was at Burnley [1990/91], because we had such good support, especially away from home when we'd play at these smaller grounds like Rochdale or Scarborough and we'd take 6,000 Burnley supporters, the atmosphere was unbelievable. It does really help you when you've got fans on top of you, and you feel the atmosphere, whereas Tuesday night at Scunthorpe and there's 1,500 there, you know you've got to motivate yourself.

When I was at Barnsley, I remember Bobby Collins telling me, 'You're playing in the reserves tonight,' it was me and Wyldey [Rodger Wylde] up front on a Tuesday night and it was freezing cold, raining. Anyway, the next day I got a call from Joe Royle, he said, 'We've agreed a fee with Bobby Collins, are you interested in coming to Oldham? I've seen you play loads of times, I know your ability but I just wanted to make sure about your commitment, and I was at the game last night. Wasn't it cold? I was freezing in the stands but you gave everything for 90 minutes, other players were going through the motions –

that's why we're having this conversation.' So you've got to make your own effort, even if there's hardly anybody watching – you never know who's watching.

### *So you went to the coldest ground in the country!*

It was freezing, the coldest ground I ever played at, but that's why we won so many games, because teams would come and mentally didn't fancy it. It was bleak, Boundary Park.

# Nigel Gleghorn

Nigel was born in 1962 and joined First Division Ipswich Town from Seaham Red Star, where he combined football with working as a fireman. He went on to make over 500 appearances in a long career with several Football League clubs.

***You had an unusual route into the Football League – can you explain how that came about?***

The story goes, I was in the fire brigade – I'd been out of work for a year during one of the downturns that we have, and I got into the fire brigade at 19 and went and played football for my local side in the Drybroughs Northern League. I wanted to play at the highest standard I could and that was a good standard at the time, people like Alan Shoulder went straight out of the Northern League to play for Newcastle in what was then the First Division. I went on trial [at Ipswich], I was on trial for about two years, I couldn't make my mind up. I hadn't seen the manager [Bobby Ferguson] in all that time, I just played in the reserves, and then I finally met the manager. I played against Notts County, and played really well so he invited me down to Portman Road and asked me if I wanted to sign. At the time, I wasn't going to because I'd just gone to the fire brigade and had a secure job.

Negotiations went a little bit like: 'how much do you get in the fire brigade?' – I think it was £140 a week – 'I'll give you £200 a week' – no, no – and he went 'I'll give you £250 a week and a two-year contract.' I said 'two years is not enough,' so he went 'I'll give you £5,000 to sign on.' In those days that was a lot of money to me, I'd never seen that sum in my life and in the end I wasn't going to sign, he went 'what do you want? You either walk out of here a fireman or a footballer, which do you want?' So I pitched something – I thought he would say 'you're coming from non-league mate, who do you think you are?' – 'I want £300 a week' (that was doubling my fire brigade wage), 'a three-year contract and I want £10,000 to sign on,' thinking he was just going to laugh at me, and he just went 'right, sign here.' That was sort of how negotiations went in that era, for me anyway!

Then I signed, and I had to work my notice in the fire brigade – there's a story, I got a phone call in August, I'd done a lot of training and Ron Gustard, who was on my watch, an older fireman, shouts upstairs: 'Nige, there's a phone call for you!' I went 'yeah, who is it?', because no-one ever rang the station, and he said 'it's Bobby Ferguson from Ipswich' and I thought 'you're just taking the mickey because I've signed.' So I came down and it was actually Bobby Ferguson, and he asked 'are you fit?' I said 'yeah, I've been doing some training,' because this was in August, I was due to finish on the 28th before the Bank Holiday, and this was somewhere in between that. So he said 'right, we've got injuries so get fit, get fitter, because you could be playing at Anfield next week against Liverpool.' I thought he was having a laugh! He was deadly serious, he said 'if Trevor Putney doesn't get fit, you'll be playing against Liverpool next week.' Luckily I think Trevor and Frank Yallop got fit, and I missed out on a 5-0 drubbing with Ian Rush scoring a hat-trick. It would have been nice to make my debut against Liverpool, who were then the best team around in Europe. I had to wait, I got injured about a week after I went down there, an ankle injury, and I had to wait to make my debut at Highbury instead.

### *What are your memories of making your debut?*

Off the pitches in the Drybroughs Northern League to Highbury – it was surreal, I thought I was just going along to make the numbers up. So I was looking around the fabled marble halls of Highbury, I went to the toilet and I heard Bobby say 'where's the fireman?' He came and pushed the door open and said 'you're substitute!' Right, OK, I was shaking for a minute. So I was substitute at Highbury, they only had 12 players in those days, only one sub. I was sat next to Terry Butcher, the England captain, having come from the fire brigade, from the Drybroughs Northern League to Highbury, watching Charlie Nicholas, Paul Davis, John Lukic, Viv Anderson, all that lot playing who I used to watch on *Match of the Day*! I'm watching from the dug-out and Kevin Steggles went down injured after six minutes, so I learnt lots of things that day – 1) never just have your shin pads in your hands, make sure you've got them on, 2) never wear one of those big cat-suits, because I couldn't get it off, my hands were shaking and I couldn't get hold of the zip – Terry Butcher actually had to unzip me. Once I got on, I was fine – that was my debut, at Highbury! It was surreal, I can't actually put it into words, I felt like I was in a dream somewhere. After all the knock-backs I'd had as a kid, to finally make it was really good, really nice feeling.

I remember going in on Monday, and Ipswich being the club it was – the three years at Ipswich shaped me for the rest of my career, it was so professional, the people around the place and Bobby Ferguson, Charlie Woods, Brian Owen – so professional, the way they did things, it just rubbed off on you. Then you had the old pros, Terry Butcher – I was there for a year with him – Steve McCall, Ian Cranson, George Burley was around for a few months while I was there. They taught you how to be a professional footballer, what it meant and what you had to do to be a professional footballer. I remember coming in on the Monday and looking at the squad, and I was down for extra training on the Monday afternoon with the reserves! So I'd made my debut at Arsenal, and as I walked in Peter Trevivian, who was the youth team coach, pushed me against the wall – and this has stuck with me forever – and he said 'don't ever think you're a footballer until you've made 100 appearances.' Down to earth, kept my feet on the ground, a proper club. He wasn't aggressive, he just made sure that I knew where I was, that I hadn't made it.

I learned a load at Ipswich, it was a smashing club, both in and out of favour. When John Duncan came, he didn't fancy me at all, could only see that I didn't have any pace, couldn't see anything beyond that. That led to me not playing very much, at the time I had a hernia, didn't want to go and get it sorted until I was back in favour but it never quite worked out with John Duncan, didn't play my style of football, couldn't see through the fact that I wasn't quick. I got lucky – I'd made nearly 100 appearances for Ipswich over those three years – Tony Book came down with Ken Brown from Manchester City to watch Wayne Biggins play for Norwich in the reserves against Ipswich. With Ipswich I'd had a relegation in my first season, by I think a point, and then I played in the first-ever play-offs against Charlton, over two legs. I'd had the downs with Ipswich, even though there were a lot of plusses, and then the John Duncan scenario, so when Ken and Tony Book came down to watch Wayne I didn't realise, I was just playing and had a decent game but Mel Machin, manager of City, was looking for a left-sided midfielder so they took me and Wayne.

We moved up in the 88/89 season and it was a no-brainer for me – I actually took a pay cut to come to City, because obviously when a manager signs you, he sees something that he likes. The pace thing would come back with Mel, but in a very different way. With City, I think I played 42 games in one season, scored 13 goals but I only made 26 full appearances, the rest were as sub. It was a really good season – we started badly, picked up and then at the end of the season we needed to win a game to go up, to get promoted to the Prem. We were 3-0 up against Bournemouth and Vic Callow gave a penalty in the 98th minute for an equaliser – that would have got us up. So we drew, and our last game of the season was against Bradford away, we needed a point – if we got beaten and Palace won by five, they would go up in our place. We went 1-0 down after 20 minutes, we played really well that day, that many City fans got in, I don't know how they did it, and we scored in the last five minutes of the season to get a 1-1 draw which took us up at the expense of Palace.

We managed to get promotion that season, we really enjoyed it – the big part about that season was that it was such a good dressing-room, the players were all so together. That's what helps so much – Ipswich was a really good dressing-room – this was a mixture of young lads who'd come through and had Manchester City in their blood, Glyn Pardoe helped to bring through Paul Lake, Paul Moulden, Jason Beckford, Andy Hinchcliffe, there were lots of them in that squad, with a few signings that Mel had made and a couple of older heads. Everybody got on, it was a really good atmosphere, everyone played to enjoy and win things, and that's what we did. We ended up getting promotion, and deserved to do so.

This is where the pace thing comes in again – because I'm left-footed, I always got stuck out wide left – well, I was never a winger. Wingers are either tricky, or they've got some pace. So having been promoted, I remember being on holiday in Portugal, on a train coming back from Lisbon. Of course there were no mobile phones in those days, so I bought a newspaper and our first game of the season was Liverpool, away at Anfield! I couldn't wait to get back, got myself in the reckoning and I played at Anfield, first game of the season. It was 1-1 for about 65 minutes, Andy Hinchcliffe had scored, but then Liverpool won 3-1 in the end and showed their class – I think they were champions. We were out on our feet, we'd given a good account of ourselves having not signed too many players – Ian Bishop was one of them. This was the difference between Mel and John, because Mel identified the things I could do, beyond the fact I had no pace, and used them as best he could. I played against Liverpool, we got beaten by Southampton with Matt Le Tissier playing – I scored in that game – the next game was Tottenham at home, and he dropped me.

He got an offer from Birmingham for me, my old manager Bobby Ferguson had gone there, and Mel just pulled me aside and told me 'I can't promise you a game.' I said 'I don't want you to promise me a game, I just want you to give me a fair crack, which you have done last season – I've earned what I've done.' He said 'we've had an offer, it's up to you, I don't mind – you can stay if you want to or you can go and talk to Birmingham.' He was upfront, and I quite liked that. It was my decision, dropping two divisions and you might see that as a mistake, but having played 42 games for City I then played over 170 games for Birmingham, had a promotion scoring the goal that took them up from the First to the Championship against Shrewsbury. Again, a good dressing-room with lads who'd come through – Paul Tait, John Frain, Ian Clarkson – and Martin Thomas, Trevor Matthewson, a couple of signings that were made. This was with Dave Mackay, but then he left and Lou Macari came in.

Now Lou's a manager who people will either like or dislike, I always got on fine with him. He took me to Stoke later on, but at Birmingham I had a promotion, a Wembley appearance in the Leyland DAF. Lou Macari used to work you so hard, it was untrue – his teams were noted for going for the whole 90 minutes, and I could see why because we ran, and ran, and ran! He got us really fit and he was good at spotting footballers that would fit in his team. He once ran us all up to Aston Villa's training ground, this was about five or six miles, and said 'just have a look in there. That's what you get when you're good footballers! Now come on, let's run back.'

When I'd first signed from Manchester City, where it was so well organised – Mel's training was excellent, I always enjoyed his sessions – I'd come down to Birmingham and we went for a run round the streets and then went into this little park. The lads called it 'dogshit park,' it had a little copse of trees and five-a-side goals where the pitch was worn out, it wasn't even cut or anything. I thought 'my God!' We had a 10-a-side on this and the ball was kicked into the woods – I just turned to walk away and Lou shouts 'play on!' while five professional footballers run into the copse, getting scratched and twigs snapping... I just thought 'what have I done?' He had a way of doing things, and he was successful with it, we got to Wembley. You had to know how to read him, that's all. We trained, and we went on to beat Tranmere 3-2 – John Gayle got two and Dean Peer got the other.

Then Terry Cooper came, he finally sold me to Stoke for £100,000 so I re-joined Lou. That first season at Stoke we had five derbies, another good dressing-room – this was quite a hard-nosed changing-room though. We had some really good footballers – this was one of Lou's big qualities, he knew how to put a team together. Just because he used to work you hard, to get you as fit as possible, people forget that he actually had some good footballers in his teams. Lou was very good at spotting a striker – in that period of a few years I played with Paul Peschisolido, Dave Regis, Mark Stein, Kevin Russell, Mike Sheron. When you look at the centre-forwards he had, he knew how to get goals. He also knew how to get a real resilience in there, and in the end that's how you get yourself a promotion. I actually scored the goal against the great Peter Shilton that took Stoke up at the end of the season. We scored after four minutes and Peter Fox made a stupendous save to keep us in the game. Good memories.

I've had some great clubs and worked with some good people. There are actually a lot of good people in football, there's just the odd thing that happens and footballers get tainted – the majority are good people who get on with what they have to do. I signed for Burnley after that, had two years there at another smashing football club, with Adrian Heath and John Ward. Then Chris Waddle came, who again didn't fancy me – it wasn't him, but Glenn Roeder made a bit of a comment in a massive team meeting with everybody there. I just felt at the age of 35, 36 he might just have pulled me aside and said 'look, we're not going to keep you after this season' – then as a good pro, you look after them because they've been straight with you. I went on loan to Northampton with Ian Atkins, and I went on loan to Brentford with Micky Adams. I scored a couple of goals here and there but really my career fizzled out a little bit. I had the opportunity to go to Chester for two years but chose to go into teaching if I could – that's what I wanted to do. So there's a quick snapshot of 560 games!

It's difficult just to single out one club because they all leave you with something. Even though I've had a relegation, and a couple of play-offs with Ipswich and Stoke, that's dispersed with a couple of promotions and a Wembley appearance. Unless you're at a top club, you can't take it for granted, but 560 league and cup games in 13 years – it's quite hard work, but it's a great life, I've been very lucky in my life. All great clubs, I couldn't say anything against any of them.

You could say Ipswich going down is not successful, but having sold Thijssen, Muhren, Wark, Butcher, Gates, Brazil and bringing in some really talented young players – Jason Dozzell, Mark Brennan, Kevin Wilson and one or two others – you can see that going down by a point wasn't actually that bad. Then making the play-offs was a success, the next year. There's been ups and downs all the way through, and that's what makes a career good, otherwise it'd get a bit boring.

It gives you character – when you play football, you've got to be driven – it's not easy being a professional footballer. There's good trappings, especially nowadays, but if you ask me whether I would rather play now or then... I'd like to play now because of the sports science that might help you, but then I wouldn't trade off any of my 550 games because now I might only have played 300 – I'd rather have played when I did because I enjoyed playing so much. In the years at Birmingham and Stoke, injury-wise, I think I missed two games and I was dropped for six, so I only missed eight games in seven years or something.

### *And there was next to no rotation, even for cup games?*

You didn't want rotation, because that gives someone else a chance to take your place. I suppose in many ways, squads were smaller but once you were left out, it was more difficult to get back in. You had to earn your place, and keep it. Managers didn't just change teams, or think 'you've done 60 minutes – here's 30 for someone else' – you wanted to play every minute of every game. Players are no different now, they still want to play, they just have a different mentality to being left out. Then again, we don't see what goes on behind the scenes, I'm sure there'll be some upset somewhere along the line, 'cause you want to play.

### *What are your earliest football memories?*

My first memories of football as a kid – I came from a mining town in the north-east, Seaham Harbour, which has produced a few footballers. Back then, Terry Fenwick played for England, Brian Marwood, to name a couple. Quite a few had gone to play for Newcastle and Sunderland. So I started playing at seven years old, from the school yard. I went through those years playing with some good footballers, because in those days that was all you did, there were no other distractions, it was sport and we played loads of football – on the dump, everywhere we played. I remember the big change-over from junior school to senior school and I'm an August birthday, I was always little and skinny. There was a lad, extremely good footballer, who I thought was better than me even though I'd been the best at my school – I thought he was better because he was bigger than me, basically. So when I went for trials, I went as a goalkeeper and I got in the school team as a left-back. I didn't challenge, when I was asked where I played I said 'left-back or goalkeeper.' I didn't put left midfield or left centre mid, which is where I ended up with Stoke – I ended up in the position I should have been all along when Stoke moved me in one. I finally got into midfield as a more forward-thinking player later on (about year 8).

I used to go and watch Red Star now and again when I was a kid, they were in the Wearside League then, but I'd rather be playing than watching. I was in the school football team for my year, the year above and the year above; the rugby team for my year and the year above; and the basketball team for my year and the year above. So when the teacher asked 'where's your homework?', it was generally on the basketball court, the rugby pitch or the football pitch. I was out playing sport all the time. Loved it.

I think a turning point is when you accept that you're not going to get there. My two brothers are very talented footballers, and there came a time I had trials at Wolves, Sheffield United, Newcastle and then Middlesbrough when I was 18. At that time, that's when I accepted that I wasn't going to be a footballer. I thought my careers teacher was going to be right – he sat me down and said 'right Gleghorn, what are going to do with your life now you're leaving school?' I said 'I'm going to be a footballer, sir.' He went 'there's only one in two thousand make it. You're not going to be a footballer. You've played that much sport, your exams aren't very good – go down the pit like your dad.'

So there was an acceptance at 18 that I might not make it, but I always had this drive to play at the highest level I could. When I left junior football I was already playing at Seaham Red Star, at 17, which was quite unheard-of at that time. Sometimes you need that little bit of luck, and it wasn't me playing, but it was my manager, Larry Phillips, who was a fireman. He used to scout all over Durham, and he was in the foothills of the Durham Dales somewhere watching Brandon United play when a bloke started chatting to him. It was John Carruthers, a scout from Ipswich, looking for a left-sided player. He told me 'you don't need to look any further, we've got one at my club – come and watch him.' I was 19, 20. He came and watched me playing on a Sunday morning for a team called Burton [?] Victoria, I scored a hat-trick and straight away he sent me off for trials. If Larry hadn't been at Brandon that night, I'd probably be retiring as a fireman right now. That little bit of luck, somebody else in the right place at the right time, gave me a little break and that's what you need at times.

### It's hard to imagine someone making that jump now

It was more common then – Chris Waddle came from Tow Law, Stuart Pearce from Wealdstone, Vinny Jones, Ian Wright –

quite a few came out of the non-league set-up. The competition in non-league then was fierce, it wasn't diluted. The squads in professional football were generally about 16 hard-nosed pros, 6 kids and a few who might just get there. They weren't massive, and then you had some kids who would play in the reserves – this was a big thing, the reserves were usually 6 pros who weren't playing or coming back from injury and a few young 'uns getting taught the ropes – that's how it was done then. At Manchester City at times I played in the reserves with some good young players – the likes of Paul Warhurst, Ashley Ward who went on to have very good careers. They were coming through at the time and as a pro, you had to teach them. A good pro can teach loads in a game.

### *Who was your favourite team, and players, growing up?*

I was a Sunderland fan but it was more about playing. I used to go and watch Sunderland now and then but generally I played on a Saturday, and I had a paper round on a Saturday night. I remember when Sunderland had got relegated (again!) and Jimmy Adamson had brought all the kids in – Shaun Elliott, Kevin Arnott, Gary Rowell. I thought 'I'll go and watch them,' it was an evening game and I think they beat Middlesbrough 4-0, so I thought 'I'll have a bit more of that!' The next game they beat West Brom 6-something, and then someone else by 4, and these kids were just on fire. The things I remember about going to Roker Park, getting off the train and walking across the bridge where the new ground is now – when you walked in, the pitch was just unbelievable. The lights reflected the green of the grass – it's great playing floodlit football, I love it when the lights are on, I think it's absolutely magnificent. That was something else! I scored at Roker Park for Manchester City, at the Fulwell End where I used to stand.

### *Who were your most difficult opponents, or the best players you played with or against?*

The most difficult opponent I ever had was Denis Irwin. I played against Denis about four times and I'm still waiting to be let out of his pocket! He was quick, too quick for me, he wasn't very big so I thought I'd be able to bully him in the air, but actually he could jump as well. He was my toughest opponent. Players I've played with? There's too many to mention, 'cause they all have different qualities. Steve McCall, when I first played pro football he played left-back and I was left midfield, he would just clear up all the mess I made and help me out, give me the ball. I learned loads from him, he was a massive influence. You've got to be good to be a pro footballer, there's not much margin for error, even if you're playing in the Second Division, you're still one of only a few thousand who are playing football. It's tough to say, having played with Mark Stein, Paul Lake, Terry Butcher, Kevin Keen at Stoke, Toddy Orlygsson, it depends what you're looking for.

I played against the Newcastle team, we got a thrashing 4-0 down at the Vic off them – Peter Beardsley was playing, Ginola, Albert, Srnicek, Warren Barton, Watson and I think it might have been Asprilla up front. That's the best team I've ever played against, and that's saying something because at Stoke we'd gone to Chelsea in the League Cup, played against Ruud Gullit. We also played in the Anglo-Italian Cup against Parma, Udinese, against Hagi – he was at an Italian club at the time – when I was playing for Birmingham. I've played against Stefan Effenberg as well, and when you look at [Manchester] United's team that Stoke played, with Bryan Robson, Hughes, Pallister, Bruce, Sharpe, McClair, Kanchelskis... it's very tough to pick a player. The only one would be if I'd played against Pelé – he was the person I used to watch the most.

Glenn Hoddle – he would be un-buyable in this era now, 'cause he could do everything. But around that time you had a lot of flair players, Charlie George was another one, Leeds had Lorimer around the 70s, players who were a massive influence on my football. In my day you had *Match of the Day* on a Saturday, and *Midweek Sports Special* on a Wednesday – and that was it. So my mum and dad used to let me stay up on a Wednesday to watch it, quite late, 10 or 10:30 if I could get up for school. The teams in those days – Leeds, Chelsea, Liverpool, Arsenal, all had top players. The team that Sunderland beat in the [1973] FA Cup Final, Jones and Allan Clarke, then they had Bremner and Giles, Hunter, Madeley and Cherry at the back, Lorimer. They had an excellent side, but so did many other teams. Peter Osgood was a class player for Chelsea. Through the 70s, those were the types of players I used to watch. I wouldn't miss *Match of the Day* or *Midweek Sports Special*. If I was being a bit critical of today's football, I think it's much of a muchness, teams play the same way – that's about the only criticism I could have, because the players are ultra-fit, they're technically gifted, they make the game look easy. I just think there's no surprises, it's all pattern play, no-one tries anything different.

Not to say that some of the players in the 70s and 80s weren't technically gifted, because they were – and the pitches they had to play on... I remember at Coventry, Highfield Road, it didn't have a blade of grass on it! The Baseball Ground, I played there on pretty heavy surfaces – and they had good players earlier, with Francis Lee and Alan Hinton, Roy McFarland and that 70s team. So there were some really technical players, it was just a different era, and how things have evolved. But I could cope with the pitches, I was used to it from non-league, I hadn't been spoiled, just got on with it – it's a cliché, but it's the same for both sides.

***I wanted to ask about the physical contact – from a fan's perspective, we seem to have gone from one extreme, where there was not enough protection for the more skilful players especially, to the other, where free-kicks are given for virtually any physical contact. What's your take on that?***

Watching football, I'd like to play now because you don't get kicked! It could be classed as more cynical now but they could kick you quite openly in those days, now everything's professional fouls which break the game up. I think there's got to be a balance, the outlawing of the tackle from behind was fair, it's a dangerous tackle, players can get hurt – it's a good law that was passed. Referees need to start refereeing games, and the players that fall over, they're the ones that should start getting booked. I also think they need to do something about that professional foul that breaks the game up. People used to speak to me about how Barcelona played football – in possession, they were outstanding with Xavi and Iniesta – it wasn't a fair mix, because if you got out of their press, they'd just foul you. I remember someone talking to Jose Mourinho about Deco, saying 'he had a good game today' and Mourinho said 'yes, he knew exactly when to foul.' If someone's through on goal, you might bring them down, but if it's high up the pitch, to stop a counter-attack, it's just cynical. There needs to be something done about that, to make football more of a spectacle. People do go down too easily, I call it cheating, there's no other word to put to it.

***What about the plastic pitches, how did you find playing on them?***

Just before they ripped it up, I played on the QPR one, there were tears in it that they'd just left. When it was folded back – well today you'd probably see better astroturf in somebody's garden, it was just sand. My ankles and hips were aching like mad after that game, and I was only 23, 24. Oldham's was a bit better but did give them an advantage. [At Birmingham] We played them in the FA Cup with Earl Barrett, Frankie Bunn, Nicky Henry, Ricky Holden, a really good side. We drew 1-1 at our place, I scored against Jon Hallworth, who I was at Ipswich with, and we got a thrashing up there. It did give them an advantage, because back then we couldn't source an astroturf pitch to play on, there weren't many about. The pitches now are great, I think it's 40% grass and 60% weave, absolutely brilliant. St George's Park and the top training grounds, they're all like that – one of them's like Wembley.

***Another major change is the grounds themselves. You played in front of the Kippax at Maine Road, the Boothen End at the Victoria Ground; how conscious are you as a player of the noise from the crowd and the atmosphere in the ground?***

It is different now, at big clubs you get a lot of 'day fans' who come in. I was lucky enough to do a lot of radio work for Stoke and Man City, I've watched City evolve over the years into the sort of side they are now. As they've got better and better, it's got a bit quieter in the ground 'cause their expectations are different. The really big games, that's when City fans really come into their own now. When they're playing smaller teams, they don't expect to get beaten. The big games, Cup games, that's when it gets back to how it used to be, when I was in front of the Kippax – it used to hold about 20,000, the Kop at Birmingham, the Boothen End – those big standing terraces, there was real noise coming from them. We need to be very careful that we don't make football too sterile, I think they should bring back some standing – they do it at Dortmund, thousands on that Kop – if they can do it safely, I think there should be an end at every ground where people can stand up. It is a different experience, you get moved along with it all, the noise was phenomenal.

You can't go back with rose-coloured spectacles all the time, I remember going to Roker Park and you couldn't get to the toilets properly, nothing really worked. The facilities were shocking to say the least, and you accepted them as a fan. Now the clubs have done a lot to make the fans paying customers and have a different experience on a match-day. We've got to remember the world's changed, youngsters are different, they've got other distractions that can take them away from the game compared to when we were younger, and that's why you've got to sell the game well. It's really sad that the old Vic's gone, the Brit's a lovely stadium but it's not the Vic. A lot of the old grounds are gone, Roker Park went – I've been to the Stadium of Light a couple of times, it's a fabulous stadium but it's not Roker Park. They're new stadiums, to give people different experiences. If they bring back standing, I think that'll be a better experience.

# Derek Goodier

Derek was born in 1938 in Talke, Staffordshire and has had a keen lifelong interest in the game, as player and watcher, following Stoke City over nine decades.

***Can you tell me about your earliest experiences of football – playing and watching?***

My earliest recollection of watching football was 1943 when I was five years old at Stoke, the Stan Matthews era during the war. I had a lull and then I started watching Stoke regularly with my dad which would be about 1947 – aged eight, I was watching them then. I was playing football too, a junior, I was nine, eleven; no such thing as coaching or anything like that. No such thing as goalposts or nets. I'd got an old ball stuffed with grass and you just went along like that. No such thing as football boots, you were barred from playing football if you wore clogs so you had to play in your bare feet or stocking feet, and that was my first introduction to football. Nothing like grass – mostly cinders, gravel, red ash or tarmac if you were lucky. No niceties at all. Nothing like eleven-a-side, it was more like thirty - to fifty-a-side. No referee, no nothing. Whoever got the ball was very lucky.

***And how did you begin playing organised football, was that through school?***

At school – when I went to the senior school because there was no organised sport at junior school. I was eleven, twelve when I went there. It stood you in good stead playing with plenty of people because it seemed as though you had more space. Still no strips or anything like that until later on, when you came into the last two years at school. I had a pair of football boots by then. There was no such thing as socks but I'd got a pair of boots and a heavy old 'casey' [football] which was a number five – as young lads you could probably move it about ten, twelve feet. You wouldn't move it any farther. It was too heavy and if it was wet you didn't move it ten or twelve feet, it was more like six. It was a big case ball because the case balls then came in different sizes. That was the number five size, that was the big one. All leather with a rubber inner tube inside and a lace. When you tried to kick it and you didn't quite catch it right – there was no such thing as trying to volley it as a young lad because it would break your ankles. You couldn't head it, you couldn't catch it on your chest because the ball was just too heavy, too big. So you progressed from there and when you were about fifteen you started getting the hang of it. You went forward from there and joined a team, and if you were good enough you were picked and I was picked at sixteen to play for Kidsgrove United.

It was an introduction to something very hard because football then was really, really, hard. There were no questions asked, you just had to get in on it and you spent more time flying through the air or being kicked. But you learn – you had to learn the hard way. You had to be clever, you didn't stand about, you got the ball to your feet and did your best and tried to get round somebody and beat 'em and that was how it was played, football then. If you hadn't got the skill, you'd get all the knocks so you learned skills pretty quick.

### *What position did you play and who decided that?*

I played at inside-right with the junior team and as I came into the senior team, the first team, I was moved out onto the wing because it afforded me more protection, you had more space. In midfield you had wing-halves and inside-forwards and defenders all wanting to kick you, so I wasn't big enough for that. I wasn't strong enough and I wasn't big enough. I suppose I'd got the heart to do it but I was kicked from pillar to post so I was put out onto the wing and that's where you learn more skill, because you've got more time so you could take people on. The art of playing football in my younger days was beating somebody with the ball, not getting the ball, holding onto the ball a minute, and then passing it – passing the buck as I call it –

to somebody else and you are just passing it about the field aimlessly with nothing at the end of it. It's not my idea of what football's about.

***Who were your favourite players? Was there a player who inspired you, who you modelled your game on, or that you would have looked up to at that age?***

Well, the players that you looked up to at that age when you were playing out on the wing were Stan Matthews on the right wing and Tom Finney on the left wing. And if you could get anywhere near one-one-hundredth of what they were like, you were doing alright because they were phenomenal players. You always thought in your own mind 'I could do that' but it is very hard to throw a dummy, especially to throw a dummy to feign to go inside and go outside because you're on the wrong leg to push off. You can't do it in the same way as the professional players but you learn about it, you learn how to do it.

***And that was quite a high level that you were playing at with Kidsgrove wasn't it?***

Some moved on [to professional football] and some couldn't afford to move on. It was a time [mid-1950s] when you couldn't move on because of home commitments – then you were expected to pay in to the home finances, that was part and parcel of your life. You couldn't afford to become a professional footballer. You were very lucky if you could, so there were very few who went that way. When I first started playing football at that level, the reserves from all of the big central teams such as Wolverhampton, West Brom, Stoke – if they were coming back from injury, they were playing in the same league as I was playing in. So it was no easy task, no easy task at all.

***You were playing against professionals – were there any in particular that you remember being tough opponents?***

Johnny McCue from Stoke warned me off; he said 'don't try to be clever and you'll be alright.' So I took him at his warning and just played a normal game and come off unscathed, otherwise I think I'd have been about ten feet up in the air and learning how to fly because he was unforgiving, that bloke was. But I played against a lot of professional footballers and you learn a lot from them if you watch them because they are very clever. They are not as clever now, they are more cynical.

*To go back to watching football, you first went to Stoke, the Victoria Ground around 1943 during the war-time leagues and that continued when league football resumed. Could you just say a bit about the experience of going to a match then, how it was, where you watched the game from, the crowds etc.*

Well, the thing is when you went to Stoke and you were only small, you weren't allowed on the ends behind the goals, they were for adults only. You could go in the paddock – if you couldn't afford to go in the stand, you went in the paddock. And what happened when you went in the paddock with your parents, I was with my father, you were passed down over the crowd and put on the running track round the outside, and then you'd got the grass and then the line. So you were put down on there to watch the game. That's how you watched the game, all kids together sitting on the running track.

*So you had a close-up view of Stanley Matthews and other players at the time. I imagine it was amazing to watch him at close quarters?*

Oh yes, it was. He was a magnificent player, he was fast over ten yards, incredibly fast. Deceptively fast and the way he could drop his shoulder to feign to go right, drop it to left and go right was unbelievable. I've never seen a bloke like him, it was like the ball was glued to his foot, unbelievable player. He never got booked in his life, he was just a superb footballer. Never see the like of him again, I'm just happy that I managed to see him. Oh, he was adored at Stoke, everybody loved him at Stoke – that was what everybody went to watch, Stan Matthews. When he got the ball, the roar was unbelievable.

***My next question is about the noise and the atmosphere at the grounds. How did you find that – were the crowds particularly biased to the home team? Would they boo away players or was it a more fair-minded atmosphere?***

No, it didn't matter if he was a home player or an away player. There came some fantastic players to Stoke that I saw. It didn't matter who they were. If they were playing and they were brilliant and they did something, they were cheered. They cheered the football. They liked the home team and wanted them to win obviously, but they cheered the football. It was more about the football than having an allegiance to one club. They enjoyed the football.

***And were there any players, either Stoke (other than Stanley Matthews) or opposition that stay in your mind as being particularly enjoyable to watch?***

Yes, blokes like Len Shackleton and Ivor Allchurch, Tom Finney, people like that, ball players. Lovely, lovely players. Beautiful players, they could do anything with the ball. And we have to remember they were playing with a ball that was heavy. A ball then could weigh anything up to 7lb in weight when it was wet, I mean these balloons they play with now – unbelievable. These blokes were amazing with the skill they had with a heavy ball, heavy pitches. Pitches not to the standard as they are now. I mean, they were just like playing on a ploughed field for want of a better description, because they were always muddy – there were no training facilities, the team trained on there every day of the week, played on there on a Saturday. Probably the reserves played on there in the mid-week, so it was getting used all the time. There was never a blade of grass between the D and the goal, it was always mud and sand. It was really hard work but there were some brilliant, brilliant players.

You see in the 1950s and early 1960s you didn't go up there [the Victoria Ground] just to say 'Come on Stoke, Super Stoke,' which they were anything but. You used to go up there and say, today Len Duquemin's here with Tottenham, or Len Shackleton's here – you went to watch that player, you knew those players would respond and play – Raich Carter, you knew all the brilliant players. That's what you went to watch. That was the heart of going to football then, just to watch the others. And if you could beat that team with the star in them, then fantastic. But Stoke had their own stars. They had Neil Franklin, who's the best centre half I've ever seen in my life. He used to go through a match and not a hair on his head was ruffled. He never had mud on his shorts or anything; by God did he win some tackles, but he didn't have to go down for them. His positioning was outstanding. Different era. Different game.

During my time of watching football from the 40s to the 70s, the people you most liked to see were the goalscorers. In the 40s and 50s you had Milburn, Mortensen, Steele, Lawton, Rowley, Lofthouse, followed by Smith, Taylor, Clough and [later] Astle, Ritchie, Osgood – what a bunch of centre-forwards! And of course you had players like Greaves and Law – what price these players, and where are their equivalents now?

### *And were there any teams that stood out, which were most impressive?*

Yes, Tottenham at that time were impressive, very impressive. They were playing a style of football which was called 'push and run.' As soon as you moved the ball, you ran to another space. It didn't take out the dribbling aspect or anything like that, but you always made for a space which you never did before, because once you'd made a pass you ambled up or run up or whatever, but you never run for space. That showed you that you could run for space and make things happen, because there was nobody there to take the ball off you until people caught on to it and started man-marking. Before that it was like block [zonal]-marking, everybody marked up, and whoever came into your territory you tackled, but after that they started man-marking.

### *As the years went on, obviously you were following Stoke. Did you ever go to other grounds either to watch Stoke or to watch another team?*

I went to every ground in Division One. I went to most of them in Division Two when Stoke were relegated. I used to enjoy visiting the other grounds, some of them were great to go to. And some of the teams were really good to watch and you got an insight into football – everybody seemed to be more for football than they were for their own team. They followed the football. There was no tribalism, cat-calling and shouting at one another or anything like that; no, it was just going to watch football and the crowds were tremendous. Massive crowds, bigger crowds than you have now because it was all standing apart from the upper stands where the directors were. I mean when you talk about being on Stoke with 60,000 – I mean the old Stoke, Victoria Ground. I've been on Hampden with 100,000. I've been on Rangers ground and Celtic ground on New Year's Day at the Old Firm matches. The experience is phenomenal.

*Over the years from the fifties into the sixties, my impression is that there were less goals scored, the game became a bit more tactical and defensive. Was that your experience of watching it over the years, did you notice a change coming into football?*

Yes, I watched a decline in the skills aspect and the goals scored. At one period if a team scored four goals, you'd think that you could score five. It's all geared up now for ball possession which doesn't mean a thing. If you have 23 possessions and you score a goal and win 1-0, what is the good of possession? It's what you do with the ball. If you've got a ball, as they do now and you play it across the field all the time, it goes backwards because nobody has the nous to go forward and do something out of the ordinary – to take somebody on or a forward with the guts to run and ping in with the ball. It's been knocked out – we play the Continental method which is possession, which is a South American thing as well. Possession isn't 90% of the game, it's only one little aspect of the game. If you do nothing during possession – pointless.

*Which were your most memorable matches of that era?*

I went to Stan Matthews farewell match at the Victoria Ground [Stoke on the 28th April 1965] – it was packed. The opposition was a world squad of players including Ferenc Puskás, Alfredo Di Stéfano, Lev Yashin, Jimmy Greaves, Johnny Haynes, Jim Baxter, Cliff Jones and a host of elite players. Stan was carried from the pitch by Puskás and Yashin. Then there was Stoke's Centennial match [played at the Victoria Ground] in April 1963 against Real Madrid, the Spanish Champions, who came with their full team – Di Stéfano, Puskás, Gento and all the rest of the stars. The match ended 2-2 and before the game there was a match involving all the old players of the 30s and 40s. There was also a friendly against Santos with Pelé in 1969. Some great players.

***What are your memories of the 1966 World Cup – did you go to any of the games? What were your impressions of that tournament?***

I thought we were extremely lucky to get through at one point. When Rattin was sent off for Argentina I thought it was very lucky to get through that match. If anything we should have lost it. I went to one match, England didn't play in it – it was [North] Korea and Portugal at Goodison Park. The football there wasn't bad, it was Eusébio now I think about it, yes it was. He was a magnificent player that bloke, a big lad. You didn't knock him off the ball. He was a nice player, very nice player. But he was a bit like Ronaldo is now with Portugal, he was the player. There was nobody else. A one-man team. That man could carry them, he was brilliant.

***Just returning to Stoke, they had earlier success and they'd had Stanley Matthews but towards the late sixties/early seventies they had a successful First Division team, won the League Cup. What are your memories of the Stoke team around that period?***

They were a fantastic team. They'd got Gordon Banks in goal which was worth, well worth anything, he was the best goalkeeper I'd seen in my life. They had a good defence, a brilliant defence, and a forward line that was equal to anything. They could play your Manchester Uniteds and all of them off the pitch. They were a real, real good side. And the thing was, the man who made them was a bloke [Tony Waddington] who'd only ever played for Crewe Alexandra in the reserves. He was no great footballer which just goes to show you that you don't have to be an outstanding footballer to be a good manager.

You've got to know what you are talking about and what clicks together – that's what makes football, not top names going into management.

***That team went a little bit into decline and football changed again around the time that I was a kid [late 70s/early 80s]. The crowds were falling and there was more hooliganism around. Did you have any experience of that? Were you still going regularly to games around that time?***

I was going, yes. You'd get hooliganism, it was part of the game. It spoiled football. A lot of people stopped going because of the violence, they wouldn't take their children because of the violence and language. It wasn't just on the pitch or in the stadium, it was outside as well. It was just rife with it. They had to do something with hooliganism but it will never return to how it was I don't think.

***At what point would you say the major change has been in English football, say from what we have been discussing to what we've got now?***

I think the big decline came to football, the start of it, when the [maximum] wage was changed. I know it wanted altering but it was altered too much. Now you see players who are non-entities walking away with £50 million, some are on £300,000 a week. I mean, where are we coming from? A million pounds for four games and I've seen far better players than all of these are. I think that was the start of it when George Eastham took them to court, and I think the next stage was when we decided we would bring foreign players in. Foreign players didn't want to come cheap, so wage inflation started. It's just mushroomed from there. Nobody can tell me that a football player is worth £300,000 a game.

***What about the influence of television, that was something that wasn't really there at all when you were starting to watch football – maybe the FA Cup Final would be about the only football you'd see? So what's your experience of that change?***

It was in black and white – yes. I think there's too much of it now, there's too much coverage of football, so-called football, as I call it. I think it's just a show-piece for the egos of a lot of people. I don't believe that you need all the back-room staff and all the hangers-on for a game of football. There are more back-room staff than there are players. I think the players go on and they're preening. It's all play-acting now, it's all like a soap opera. I mean if you were kicked in the old days, you stopped down and if you couldn't get up, you stopped down and somebody would carry you off. Not with a stretcher, they'd just carry you off. But when you were injured in the old days, the trainer used to run on with a sponge and a bucket of cold water. When you saw him coming on a frosty day, you got up. You didn't want that round you. But now one minute they're rolling round in agony for the sake of television, and the sake of getting people booked and sent off. All to do with showbusiness. And I just can't get my head round it at all. One minute they're there in agony, as though they've broken their leg and as soon as the ref's gone or he's got a card out or booked him or whatever, he's up again and he's as right as rain. Now I call that cheating. I don't like the way football's gone. I've loved football all my life, but now I've come to the point where I'm watching it and I think 'switch it off' and I just don't watch it because it bores me to death.

***Could you pick a single aspect of English football that's been improved by the Premier League?***

The only thing that I can say has improved in football are the pitches, they're like billiard tables. If you can't play football on there, you'll never play football. You must be able to play football on those pitches. I mean try playing with an old 'number five' ball on a muddy pitch on a November / December's day when it's snowing, and you can't see the lines – try playing in that. I mean everything's geared to the players now, they play in bedroom slippers.

# Steve Hetzke

Steve began his career with Reading, where he became the club's youngest player to appear in a competitive match, aged 16 years and 191 days, in 1971. He played for Vancouver Whitecaps in the NASL in 1976, and later moved to Blackpool (1982-86), Sunderland (1986-87), Chester (1987-88) and Colchester (1988-89). He has since worked for the Premier League, and at Swansea City and Crystal Palace.

***What are your earliest football memories – can you remember a particular game on TV, or a match you went to?***

Probably a professional game – we were friends with a couple of people in the town where we lived, Hungerford in Berkshire, and I was taken to Chelsea when I was a young lad, 12 or 13, something like that. It was a treat. This fellow was a season-ticket holder and he had three or four sons so he used to take them alternately, and he took me once or twice. It was the first time I ever went into an arena, I suppose, for football. It's going back a while – over 50 years – and in those days, it seemed a more truthful game, fairer – someone kicked you, you kicked them back. Whereas now – I don't like to use the word 'cheat,' you have players trying to sway the referee in different ways. So those were my first memories, I think it was Chelsea-Man City, and one of the best players I've ever seen, Colin Bell, who's just died [January 2021]. Up in the stand, with a full house, watching the game as a young kid, that gave me my first thoughts of football in a professional sense, in a proper ground.

### *Who was your favourite team, and players, growing up?*

When I was a young lad at home, going to school and playing football at a young age – I was lucky enough to be able to go through the ranks – my mother kitted me out in white t-shirt, white shorts and white socks. She said it was easier to boil it and get the grass stains out, so the only team at the time in white were Leeds United. That was my early days, following them – Jack Charlton, Norman Hunter, all those players, they were the ones I grew up around. There wasn't that much football on the TV in those days, so it was only really what you read in the paper and what you had comics-wise, that was my first inkling of football.

### *You played for Reading at a very early age, what was your route into professional football?*

I was playing for my local team, and my school team, at 14 or 15, and there was a scout at Reading who'd been told about me, and he came along to watch one game. Very luckily I was then asked up to the training ground, trained for two days and they signed me on as an apprentice footballer – before the YTS, or scholarships. I went up there in the June after my sixteenth birthday, signed as an apprentice and three or four months later I was playing in the first team!

I think it was more through injuries than me being a top player, but to this day I believe I'm the youngest player to start a game for Reading. That was Darlington away on a Tuesday or Wednesday evening, I think it was, travelled up on the day on a rickety old bus, travelled back the same night, seemed to take days. I can't remember too much about the game, mainly just going out there, getting through it – I did OK, didn't do anything wrong but nothing particularly outstanding either. I played another three or four games that season, and that was it. So I was lucky, I went from local football at a young age, I was fairly tall, and I was lucky enough to get signed on.

### *What was it like at that time for a young player in the Football League, much more physical than now?*

I played a game before I signed as an apprentice, a couple of weeks before, maybe the end of the season, I was 15 and it was West Ham away. I remember playing against a lad a couple of years older, their centre-forward, the ball was coming over and the next thing I knew, I was looking up at the sky, thinking 'what's going on here!' I got a whisper in my ear, 'look after yourself,' and from then on I did. Lucky to have been a big lad – 6'2" – but I was a gentle giant, really, I wasn't a dirty player. People wanted me to use my weight and height and strength, but I wanted to play football, not be a bully.

### *You played a summer in the North American Soccer League [1976, with Vancouver Whitecaps] – how did that come about?*

Bob Lenarduzzi was an apprentice with me at Reading, we both got signed on, and his father-in-law was maybe on the board, something like that. I was asked to go over, and spent three months there – as simple as that, in those days you could just transfer your contract over. I had my twenty-first birthday over there, I think that lasted about three weeks! Made some great friends over there, Bob is, or was, club president, his brother Sam, and probably my best mate, Brian Budd, he won *Superstars* three times but sadly he's died now. We got on great, I went back there quite a few times.

It was brilliant to go across there, I played against George Best, Eusébio, all the big stars except for Pelé. Great games, memories – it was the first time I'd played on the old astroturf, not like the 3 and 4G we have now, on the American football pitches. It was a great experience, travelling up and down the country, getting on a plane for away games.

### *You stayed at Reading for a long time, why did you decide to move on to Blackpool?*

I'd been there over ten years and I was just about to sort out my testimonial, and the next season they wanted me to sign a new contract, not give me any money, and put me on the transfer list. Another way of not giving you money, basically. I said 'hang on, I've given you ten years' – I wasn't best pleased with that, and I sought to go elsewhere. Between the end of one season and the start of the next, I was speaking to Crystal Palace, they wanted me to go up there to sign, and said 'let's leave it for a few weeks' – this was in the summer. This went on for a few more weeks, then they sacked the manager, Steve Kember, and brought in Alan Mullery, so everything's changed and the season was only a couple of weeks away, but they said, 'don't worry, we'll still sign you' – and then Blackpool came in. So I went up there and signed, I knew the manager, I'd played against him – a fellow called Sam Ellis – and Bobby Downes, they were both at Watford at the time and went up there as manager and coach. So I went to play for them, and that was just literally to get away.

It went through the tribunal system, because I'd been at the club ten years the fee was set by the tribunal at Aston Villa. Less than twelve months before that, Chelsea came in and wanted me, and they were going to pay £180,000 – Geoff Hurst phoned me up at my house, and I went 'oh yeah, OK' – but Reading wanted more money, so they lost out on that as well. The tribunal set a fee of £12,500 – that's all Blackpool paid in the end, when eight or nine months earlier they could have had £180-200,000, a lot of money in those days. That night I signed, I went back to the hotel and Palace phoned, the Chief Executive, said 'don't do anything silly, we'll send a car for you, come down and sign for us.' I said 'thanks but no thanks.' That's how I ended up there – and then we had to seek re-election the next year, because someone had been stealing tickets and doing silly things with registrations. It was an interesting time up there, got a promotion, I got into the PFA team of the year [1984/85], it was a decent club to play for – then I went to Sunderland.

***How did you find your stay at Sunderland – it was a difficult time for them, like now, at a lower level than they wanted to be?***

I think that's why they asked me, they needed a defender. They had some big stars at the time – Eric Gates, Frank Gray, Alan Kennedy, George Burley, a lot of people went there. Lawrie McMenemy was the manager at the time, he tried to do what he'd done at Southampton, get some experienced boys in, but it didn't work for him. I'd have loved to have gone there at an earlier age, the place was excellent, but some of the players were only there for the money, in the end. It was a shame, because it's a lovely club.

**What was Lawrie McMenemy like to work with, I think he was the highest-paid manager in Britain at the time?**

I don't doubt it, because in the second season I was there [1986/87] he actually gave them back 'x' amount out of his wages, because they were calling for him. He needed a better staff underneath him, he had a chap called Lew Chatterley – nice enough, but he wasn't strong enough as a coach to work under Lawrie. I think he should have got someone like Alan Ball, who came to Colchester with Jock Wallace, and Alan was good, coaching-wise. My contract ended at the end of the season, and they didn't re-sign quite a few of us, and then I went to Chester. I would have gone back to Blackpool, but there was a small fee involved – in my vast years, I didn't go for a lot of money, no big 10% or anything like that!

I went to Chester under a fellow called Harry McNally, he was a bit like a mad professor, really, understood his football but went off the rails a little bit. I wasn't there long and then I went to Colchester, under Roger Brown, sadly no longer with us. They changed managers and then Jock Wallace came in, having been a God up at Rangers – he was different, didn't mess about with his words, he meant what he said. He got Alan Ball in, but then I finished with a knee injury, that was the end of my playing career. Very lucky to be able to do that, 500-plus games, 50-odd goals, I loved every minute of it!

**Was Jock Wallace still doing the fitness stuff then, running up sand-banks?**

No, he didn't do too much of that, I think he'd realised that the science was just starting to get involved, on the fitness side. He was quite strict but I thought he was great, I'd have loved to have played under him in his heyday, he would have been excellent. Hard, but if you did your work, he'd reward you accordingly.

### *How were your transfers negotiated – did you have an agent?*

No, there were very few agents, sometimes the manager almost helped you out, but I was always of the mind that if I have someone beside me, doing my talking for me, who's paying him? Well, if I do my own talking, then I can have his bit as well as the club's – not that there was a lot of it about. I wasn't a money person, I could probably have got a lot more money out of where I went, but I was just happy doing what I loved doing. The wages weren't massive either, I probably wasn't on much more money than people doing good jobs. I never used to worry about that, but maybe I should have done, made a bit more money.

The agents were there, they were in and around the game, but only for the top players. So now you'll have agents all the way down, even National League players, but then they weren't around the lower divisions, only the First Division, until people realised they could make some money. The wages now are fantastic, even going down the divisions. There are a lot of what I'd call mediocre players – and I'm not decrying them, get as much as you can – getting a hell of a lot of money for what they do. I think people could relate to you a little more because you didn't earn those vast amounts, they'd accept if you'd had a bad day – whereas now, I think they leave themselves open to criticism. If they don't run around, don't do what they should be doing, and they're earning six figures, they're always going to get stick – more so than they did in my day. We got enough stick from the terraces anyway!

### *Over the course of your career, who were your most difficult opponents, and the best players you played with and against?*

I was lucky to play against quite a few – people like Dalglish and Rush, they weren't too shabby, were they? When you play against people like that, I think you have to show them respect by playing your game as well, not just going and kicking them. We had some very good players, Paul Stewart when he was at Blackpool, he went on to Tottenham and Liverpool. Justin Fashanu, Mick Harford, you knew you were going to be up against it, they were always handy – we used to say before the game, 'are we having it today?', Billy Whitehurst as well. Then, being a big lad, the smaller players, the nippy ones in and around you, luckily I was blessed with a bit of pace. No-one ever stood out, that I was worried about playing against.

Neil Webb was at Reading, he went to Portsmouth at the same time I left, also went to a tribunal, then later Man United and England – Kerry Dixon was another one who was a decent player.

***Another player you were at Reading with, Robin Friday, he's had a lot of attention since he sadly passed away – was he special?***

He was a talent, without a shadow of a doubt. It's quite funny, the bass player from Oasis [Paul McGuigan] did a book, I got a phone call and told a couple of stories about Robin. I described Robin as 'a rock star playing football' – long hair, he'd come in with his red American cowboy boots, big scarves – but he was a talent. I think you always knew that he wasn't going to be around for a long time. Not always the best of trainers, used to like a drink, the odd drug now and again, used to spend his money for fun – got paid on a Friday and was probably done by Friday afternoon! He was obviously someone a bit different. I was lucky to play in the same team as him. Outside afterwards, he was his own person, used to go back up to London, but he was a nice enough lad, but I don't think he was ever going to be around a long time.

He was a real fans favourite, he used to do things, I remember one game he scored and jumped on a copper's back, put his hat on, that type of thing. The crowd loved him, and he was good, he had skill, scored a goal that even the referee [Clive Thomas] applauded. Rightly so, he changed games at times, but he was a bit off-the-wall, he had that rock star air.

***A player of his time, maybe, he wouldn't have fitted into today's game?***

I don't think he would have taken to the nutrition and sports science, no! We were on a pre-season run one day, and he wasn't the best of distance runners – nor was I, but he was even further behind than me – and the next minute, he was on a double-decker bus going past: 'see you, lads!' He'd jump off a hundred yards from the ground. A character to say the least.

### *Would you say there were more of those type of players around in that era – people like Stan Bowles, Rodney Marsh, Tony Currie?*

All those, fantastic – you seemed to get a lot more characters, whether that's because of the changes in the game now, I don't know – how they played, how they trained. It's changed, how Wenger turned players like Tony Adams and Paul Merson around from the drinking squads to different things. It was always going to change, but for me it's changed in a way that fans can't quite get to grips with as much, with the characters, as they would have done in the past. People like Cantona, they can latch on to, you didn't know what was going to happen next but he could do both, he could be a character and do it on the pitch as well. I'm not so sure they're around now.

### *And who were the best managers you worked with, or the ones you related to best?*

The managerial style for me was a fellow called Maurice Evans, he was at Reading as a player and a manager [later Oxford], who basically gave you a pat on the back if you played well, and if you didn't, he told you. He was very quiet, not a ranter, but then another like Sam Ellis, who was a ranter and raver, he'd get the hairdryer out but you knew if you were doing the right things. Both totally different, then in Vancouver, Eckhard Krautzun, he was more like Maurice Evans, studying the game and telling you if you didn't play well, it was because of this or that. More scholars of the game, I suppose, who understood it and put it in different ways.

The other managers – Lawrie was different, he managed players rather than on the pitch, I think at Southampton they managed everything for him on and off the pitch, with Mick Channon and people, but it didn't work up at Sunderland. So I took bits away from different people, but I think Maurice, Eckhard and Sam, if you could put the three of them together, it would have been a good mix.

***What were your most memorable experiences as a professional footballer? Could you pick a highlight of your career?***

One of the highlights was, I scored a hat-trick against Aldershot [Football League Group Cup, 1981] – scoring three goals as a centre-half is always decent! I can't really remember my first game, but just being there, walking out onto a proper ground, that was a big thing. To go from watching that game at Chelsea at 13, 14, to that, thinking I'm actually out there on that park now, I'll always remember walking out there as a 16-year-old. And the hours it took to get there and back – I think that overawed me more than the game, I had more aches and pains!

One or two goals, there was one at Luton I hit from forty yards, and there was also an own goal – it was one of those pitches where you could hardly run, we had leather studs and you had to take the top layer off, and run on the nails – I went to pass it back, the goalkeeper slipped and that was an own goal from about forty yards! Things like that I remember, rather than whole games. Getting called off in the fog at Reading – we were 3-0 up and you couldn't see from one end to the other. The first time I ran out at Sunderland, the Roker Roar, the place was full up – that was another memorable moment. Getting promotion [with Reading in 1979] at Port Vale, the pitch itself – there's a picture of us walking off after that game and there's four or five inches of mud. We were thinking, how did we even manage to play on that, let alone win promotion on it?

***The pitches you played on were very different to today's – did you feel you had to adapt your game when you played on those surfaces?***

Without a doubt, you had to play more of a long game – not just the mud, but we also played in what were virtually lakes. It was up at Sheffield Wednesday, or maybe Derby, it was just water and you literally couldn't pass the ball, you had to flick it up to kick it – I think it was a replay of a replay and it was so waterlogged, you thought it's got to be called off soon but no, we played through it. Wouldn't have even started nowadays. Some of the pitches now are carpets compared to what we were used to, same as the training grounds now, they're magnificent, better than the first-team grounds I used to play on. As the game's progressed, the ball is more on the floor now, which it just couldn't be in those days.

*The plastic pitches which came in, how did you find playing on them?*

Being a big lad, the worst one was probably down at QPR, that was like playing on concrete – we used to buy these astro-boots, basically trainers with little pimples, and you still couldn't turn on it. The bounce was absolutely ridiculous – I think it was there that Billy O'Rourke [Blackpool goalkeeper] came to get a ball on the penalty spot from the other goalkeeper, and it just bounced straight over his head for a goal. QPR, that was the worst one, Oldham wasn't far behind, Luton was OK and I think the best one was probably at Preston, only because they put more sand on it and watered it at the same time. Plastic pitches weren't the best at the time, absolutely no comparison to what they are now, which are like some of the astroturf they had in Canada, where you could play in normal studs rather than rubber. Some of the 4G's now are fantastic to play on, not that a lot of the senior pro's like them, they think their knees are going to go if they play on them a lot.

*Also tackling – as a fan, it seems to have gone from one extreme, where you could more or less get away with anything, to the other, where free-kicks are given for virtually any physical contact, players falling over. What do you make of that?*

That's what it is, players falling over. Referees ought to see this, but they don't seem to quite understand. Even when you see a fair tackle, they're just waiting for it, certain players keep falling over all the time, and they don't need to, they're good players. I don't know why – even defenders are doing it, big centre-halves getting touched and they're falling over! I suppose it must be, if I can't beat them, I'll have to join them. I don't know how we're going to get away from it, unless referees start booking people for doing it, which I thought they were in the last few seasons. This is what we talked about at the start, that honesty isn't there.

*Another major change is the grounds themselves, a lot of teams – Reading, Sunderland – have moved grounds, they're all-seater, you don't have the terraces. How conscious are you as a player of the crowd noise, do you think the atmosphere's changed over the years?*

It's a different noise, you still get noise and clubs like Palace are trying to reproduce it [with designated areas], but it did change the acoustics. Some of the bigger clubs have got less people in the stadium watching, you don't have the same noise from certain areas of the ground. One or two clubs, you could hear everything they were saying, sometimes even the players would be giggling. It was probably better away from home at times, you used to get a decent following and they were all in one place.

*From the apprenticeship you had to the way players come through the academies now, do you think there are positives and negatives in the way young players are treated?*

I think there's more positives than not, but when I went to Reading, from day one I trained with the first team because that's what the apprentices did. Scholars now won't get that chance to even train, let alone play with the first team, unless they're very good at 17, 18. It was a positive for me, I learned more in a season than some of the boys now might in four or five years. They're better looked after education-wise, in my day there were only three or four apprentices, now they've got upwards of 30 or 40, I don't know if that's a plus. They play against each other, grow up playing under-16, 17, 19, 21, 23, more than we ever did. They don't have to sweep the terraces, clean the pitch or mop out the dressing-rooms! They're looked after better, and the facilities are obviously ten-fold better.

*A lot of young players were in reserve teams, playing with and against seasoned pro's and learning from them...*

That's a good point, that doesn't happen any more. We were in the Football Combination and South-East Counties, playing against Tottenham and Arsenal, against first-team players either coming back from injury or out of the team. You gained experience from those games, and that doesn't happen, unless they get played in the Carabao Cup or that type of game. What also happened, I used to play in the South-East Counties League, under-18s in the morning, and then in the Football Combination later that day – quite a few times. I don't think any player now would play two games in a day, they'd be lucky to play two in a week!

*How do you think you would have felt about being rotated as a player?*

I don't think it's the best, some players might be happy, or not bothered about it, but if you ask most players if they want to play every game, they would say yes. I think the best teams use the least players, even to this day. Rotation is OK, but not when they're changing 50 or 60% of the team, one or two I can understand. I wouldn't have liked being rotated, playing today – I would have liked the wages, but not that!

*The opportunities for young players – there's not as many coming through, especially at the top level, despite the academies. Do you think that's to do with money, clubs and managers looking after the first team as the priority?*

There's too many players, when you're looking at the top 1 or 2% in the country, at each academy up and down the Football League and Premier League, you've got 120-150 kids across the age groups, plus what they have at different development centres. A lot of them go out of the game, it's not realistic – some of them get the chances, but most of them have only a minimal chance to make it. That's where dedication comes in – you have to have a certain amount of skill, but also be prepared to work hard, to be able to get there. The better players are also often those that worked harder. I do think that non-league football has grown immensely, it's players coming out of academies and filtered down to the National League. They're playing better football, in my day it wasn't that good, probably not even 20 years ago.

***So finally, what's your current involvement and interest in the game – would you say you still have the same passion as when you started out?***

When I first went into football, there was an old boy Jimmy Wallbanks, he was the physio at Reading – his run-on was a bladder, a sponge and bucket of dirty water – he was what they called a 'powderhall sprinter,' used to sprint for money as a young lad. He used to say to me, 'if you want to be a footballer, keep all your enthusiasm – anyone talks to you about football, talk to them back.' Well I've always talked to people about football, and I'm as keen now as I was as a 16-year-old!

# Rick Holden

Rick was born in 1964 and made his Football League debut with Burnley in 1986. He played for Halifax Town, Watford, Oldham Athletic, Manchester City and Blackpool in every division, including the Premier League. His autobiography is *Football: It's a Minging Life!* (2010) and he has since written several more titles.

*What were your most memorable experiences as a professional footballer? Could you pick a highlight of your career?*

It would have to be the Sheffield Wednesday game [May 1991, when Oldham won the Second Division title]. When you actually finally win something, especially such a long campaign after the season before, which was so gut-wrenching, that was the greatest day. The way it unfolded – being 2-0 down and thinking we'd blown it again, to come back.

And then I would say we had a successful season in the old First Division – just a pity they couldn't invest in more players, instead of selling them, getting rid of people like Redders [Neil Redfearn]. I was with him at Watford, terrific character within the club – I don't think Joe [Royle] fully appreciated what an impact he had within the dressing room, obviously Joe didn't spend much time in there. He was the life and soul in the dressing room as well – he would take the piss out of anyone but he would take it back. It was always a great laugh, and we missed him when he went. I've spoken to Joe since and he's admitted he made a mistake.

*And I think Oldham had been a good solid Second Division team for a couple of decades without spending a lot of money, without mega-rich owners – just by sensible policies, managerial stability, picking up players cheaply, which you could do then. Players would move because the wage differentials aren't anything like they are now.*

There's another thing, because of the money, you've got to question the mentality of wanting to play. I left Oldham for example at the end of my second spell because I wasn't getting a game, Sharpy [Graeme Sharp] fell out with me for some reason, wouldn't play me unless he needed a win, which happened twice, when I helped Andy [Ritchie] get a couple of hat-tricks. I said I'd rather be playing football for Blackpool's first team than on a high wage at Oldham playing in the reserves at Stalybridge Celtic – that's not inspiring at all! People said 'think about the money,' but I wasn't bloody interested in the money, that's why I went to University, so I could work after.

They're not even prepared to play at a lower level like they were in the old days, they're on a lot of money but they don't know the reality of it.

*That's another change, from reserve team football, which gave young players a chance to play with experienced professionals, to academies, where they're only playing their own age group. How does that prepare players for professional football?*

Well, it doesn't – there's a massive drop-out. It'd be interesting to find the stats and compare those that came through the reserve teams and went into first-team football to those from the academy system now. They start at the academies at 8, and I know there's a very low percentage that actually make it and are on a first-team pitch at 22 for, say, Arsenal or Barnsley. I played almost a year at Burnley in the reserves. I remember playing against Sunderland reserves, and they had people like Eric Gates and David Hodgson – they were actually encouraging me, playing for the opposition. I walked off with David Hodgson at half-time, and he said 'Well done, son. Just try this or do that' – it was a proper education, and it was tough. It really got me up to speed, playing in the reserves, but now it's like a testimonial, that type of football, no-one kicks anyone. And we used to get decent crowds at Burnley, being the fanatical club it is, we'd get a couple of thousand watching the reserves on a Wednesday night (all there with their flat caps on, and their whippets). It's difficult to put your finger on it, but I think it's gone more precious, less contact, more money, and it's a combination of those – definitely different now.

*I wanted to ask about tackling – when I watched football as a kid, there was not enough protection for the more skilful players especially, you had the tackle from behind. Now you see free-kicks given for virtually any physical contact. What's your take on that change?*

The thing is, the tackle from behind was clamped down on if the referee saw it and he was a good ref. I remember the [Littlewoods Cup] semi-final at home against West Ham, that Stewart Robson knew I was a danger, and in the first few minutes he fouled me a couple of times, bad tackles, and the ref booked him. It was only seven or eight minutes into the game, and Robson was really protesting that the ref had ruined his game! I would always take the ball, I had to say to Andy Barlow, 'I am never marked,' even if the defender's next to me with one hand in my pocket, pass me the ball – the tighter he gets to me, the better. So he did, he learned, and I would induce people to tackle me and get them booked. There was a classic at Leeds where the ref was Neil Midgley, who turned out to be a top-class comedian, after-dinner speaker. It was at Elland Road and I skipped round a couple of players when Mel Sterland came clattering in and I jumped out of the way – he came flying in like he'd been shot out of a cannon. Neil Midgley booked him, and Sterland got up protesting his innocence, saying 'I never f-ing touched him' so Midgley said 'good job you didn't, because if you had you'd be sat next to your manager now.'

So they were getting it in that late 80s/early 90s period, then it's gone to no-contact now – the pendulum has swung, but it doesn't go to the middle where you've got equilibrium, it goes right up the other side. You can't even breathe on anyone! Perfectly good slide tackles are outlawed now because they say you're not in control, but you were, if you're a professional, you knew how to do a slide tackle properly. I was always an advocate of stay on your feet as long as you can and don't dive in but sometimes, in the six-yard box or if someone's going to score, you have to throw yourself in the way of it. Does that mean it's a penalty? It shouldn't. There needs to be some judgement from the referee really, he needs to have gone through a process of refereeing at different levels, he needs to be experienced when he takes a top game on.

***I think you played 64 out of 65 games in the 1989/90 season – why do you think players need to be rested, or rotated; is the game more physically demanding now?***

Only Earl Barrett played the 65. There's a couple of things – they're trying to keep the squads happy, bigger squads so they rotate and they'll use excuses like 'I want to keep him fresh,' use physiology as a sort of smokescreen; I can remember Carlos Tevez playing hell, I think it was at Manchester United, when he was told he was going to be rested – he wanted to play but Ferguson was trying to keep everyone happy. So there's an element of that to it, but as for it being more physical, is it bollocks! The human body, if you look at records of sprinting hasn't changed much in a hundred years – do you know anyone that can do a 100 metres on a cinder track in spikes like Jesse Owens did in 1936? How many people can do a sub-four-minute mile, Roger Bannister style? The human body hasn't changed, but they've made pitches slicker, they've got them on better diets, they don't drink so much, they're more aware of the acute physiological things that have perhaps sped the game up at times. I've watched some Italian and Spanish games in the past few years and it's played at a snail's pace compared to some of the 70s games I watched. So I would say that resting players is more of a psychological and a sociological thing than a physical thing.

***What goes along with that is what they've done to the Cups – Oldham's 1989/90 Cup games against Arsenal, Villa, Everton, coming out of nowhere, were some of the most exciting I've seen.***

The glamour of it was that we were in a division below, playing these top sides who hadn't visited Boundary Park for years. That was part of the magic, because we were suddenly playing in the top flight as a second tier team – we wanted to be doing it week in, week out in the league, but the extra glamour of the Cups – I totally agree with you, they were exciting. Arsenal at home was fantastic, we couldn't wait to get into them. I'd scored the winner at Arsenal the year before for Watford when we beat them 1-0 in the old First Division, so I knew most of the Arsenal team having played against them. I'd met a few of them because I used to go out for the odd pint with Kevin Richardson, who'd been at Arsenal and he was at Watford before he went back, and one or two, Wilf Rostron and some of the Arsenal players. To play them at home, at Boundary Park, was fantastic, so yeah, the Cup's been devalued – but I notice it's not devalued when they get to the final though!

But we go back to the years before and it broke my heart as a Leeds fan when they lost to Sunderland – but they deserved to win because of the heroics of Montgomery the keeper, and it was good that Southampton repeated it against United in '76, winning 1-0, and we go up to Wimbledon winning it in '88 against Liverpool, that was good – but it doesn't happen now.

***You've touched on being a Leeds fan. What are your earliest football memories – anything that maybe influenced your career later on?***

I started following Leeds as a young kid, everybody in Yorkshire where I grew up was wearing Leeds kits – or even makeshift ones, because you could just buy a white shirt, shorts and socks and you were Leeds. My earliest memories – I remember them winning the league as a 10-year-old, in '74, as an 8-year-old winning the FA Cup against Arsenal in '72 – heroic goal by Allan Clarke, when Mick Jones injured himself and ruined his career. The biggest disappointment was '75 in the European Cup Final, when we were just absolutely cheated out of it – there's a tackle by Beckenbauer on Allan Clarke, it's the most blatant penalty you've ever seen in your life. He just bullied the referee, the Kaiser, it's unbelievable when you see the footage, he absolutely cleans him out, Clarke's done him and it's a penalty. Lorimer has a goal disallowed because Bremner's offside and he's on his arse, not interfering with play and we lost the game. I just thought 'the cheating German bastards!' – I was really bitter about that.

That era of the late 70s – it's been proved that Anderlecht got at the referee, and other ties as well – I was a big fan of Forest as well, because what they did under Clough was fantastic. I mean, that won't happen again either. It was always shrouded with a bit of jiggery-pokery, deceit going on, and I also resented that Leeds United got this label of being 'Dirty Leeds' and people still say that now. They forget that the people who started that were Chelsea against Leeds in the '70 FA Cup Final – if you look at that, the punishment that Chelsea dished out to Leeds, who were a passing side, full of skilful players, was ridiculous. I do know that Don Revie said, following that, they were going to change tactics and retaliate first – and that's what they did. So they're not going to get bullied again like that. They lost the replay at Old Trafford, and they lost too many finals by being bullied, so they did actually change tack and start dishing it out. That's why Bremner and Giles turned into assassins, and Reaney was a silent one, and Norman Hunter could do it, and Allan Clarke – they got this reputation, but it was only because they were retaliating *beforehand*.

Also I think the '74 World Cup – I didn't really remember 1970 too well, because I'd only be about six, but certainly '74, when I was ten. And then the '78 World Cup had a big influence on me because of all these long-haired Argentinians running rings round people. That was shadowed in controversy, but I know some good stories about that World Cup. It was just the way Kempes ran with the ball and things like that, it made me want to run with the ball, not necessarily dribbling, because running with the ball and dribbling it are two different skills. Running with the ball's more like a slalom effect, dribbling's making it up as you go along, like Zidane and George Best. By the time it got to '82, I was playing a lot, so everything was an influence then.

I went to a rugby-playing and a cricket-playing grammar school, so I played a lot of other sports, which I think helped me as well. Certainly playing rugby union for Wharfedale and my grammar school, nothing I met on a football pitch was going to disturb me physically.

**Did you go to games during that time?**

Yes, I used to. I cocked up once when my dad asked 'where've you been, where did you go yesterday?' – this was a Sunday – and I said 'I just played out with my mates.' So he says 'that's interesting, play out in Leeds, did you?' And he fished out a ticket which I'd left in my trousers. I'd been down to Elland Road with some older mates on the train from Skipton, and they'd paid for me to go in and watch Leeds United against Newcastle (a two-all draw). I didn't tell him because I wasn't allowed to go, I was only ten. I sneaked down into Skipton from Embsay, which was two miles, train direct to Leeds and then half a mile walk from the station to Elland Road. I got a right bollocking for that! Eventually he let me go, at about 13 I could go to games but often I was playing football or rugby myself on Saturday afternoons. At one point I got to the stage where I was playing Saturday morning rugby for the grammar school, Saturday afternoon I was playing for the village team and then progressed to the town team at football, Sunday morning was football for my team in Skipton and Sunday afternoon rugby for Wharfedale Colts – four games in a weekend, I became pretty well occupied then, coped with it and enjoyed it so I didn't get to as many games as I got older.

***You had a bit of an unusual route into the professional game, but was that always your ambition, to be a professional?***

Oh yeah, I was faffing around with trials at Bradford, and Colne Dynamos when I was 13 to 16, but I had a meeting with my dad and he said, 'look, you're going to have to do your A Levels' because football wasn't considered to be a mega-profession then – be different now – so I did. I can remember people even in my own village saying 'you've missed the boat now – look at Norman Whiteside, he's playing first team football for Man United at 16' but I didn't let it put me off, I thought 'I'll still do it.' Then when I got playing for Carnegie College first team [in Leeds] and we played friendlies midweek against professional sides, teams that had been knocked out of the FA Cup and wanted a game, they played us. We had people like Aiden Butterworth, ex-Leeds United centre-forward, on the Carnegie team, he was doing the same degree as me, and one or two other failed junior ex-pros in the squad. We had a hell of a team, Frank Harrison, he played for Middlesbrough, first team games, Halifax Town, he was the left-back and we started beating these pro teams, humiliating them at times. When we beat Burnley 4-2 at Carnegie, I'd be about 20 then, Tommy Cavanagh the manager just invited me down for training. That was the best day of my life, because I'd managed to do the education that my dad wanted me to do, and yet I'd got a toehold in the professional game at last. I think all the preparation I did, with all those games I played in on the weekends, I was strong enough and I was obviously skilful enough. I'd honed my skills by constantly playing and then it was a year in Burnley reserves, and a first team game.

Another crossroads was when Brian Miller got the job at Burnley and he wanted me to sign full-time pro forms, and I said 'I can't, I'm 2/3 of a way through my degree.' I had another discussion with my dad and he said 'no, you'd be stupid, you can't.' So I dropped out of Burnley and within five minutes Halifax Town had come in for me, and I never looked back because they were sympathetic to me, saying 'you don't have to train on this day if you've got lectures, train when you can' – I'd train at night with Carnegie's first team anyway on a Tuesday and Thursday night, we'd play on Wednesday. So they weren't worried about the physical fitness side of it, and then I signed full-time for Halifax when I'd done my degree. I always wanted to be a pro footballer but I had the academic route to go down first. They try and do that nowadays with the academies, but they're laughable. They spend more time playing poker on their computers than they do studying, from my experience.

***That transition, moving from the Fourth to the First Division [with Watford] – what was the biggest change for you; did you notice anything about the facilities, the pace of the game, was there anything that really struck you?***

It was in reverse, some of it, because when I signed for Watford I thought 'right, this is it.' We played Scunthorpe at the Old Show Ground the Saturday before for Halifax Town, we got a 1-1 draw and I got Man of the Match. A week later I'm playing for Watford against Everton, up against two England internationals, Trevor Steven and Gary Stevens, and we got beaten 1-0 but I got Man of the Match. There was absolutely no difference that I could detect in the game, not even the pace of it. It was easy! And my first inclusion in the game was I trod on Trevor Steven's foot and injured him, and then whacked the ball into Gary Stevens's bollocks in the next second, and he went down. So there's two internationals in agony on the floor, the trainers running on to help them, and I'm just standing there. I didn't do it on purpose, and I just thought 'this is no different.' When I signed for Watford, I really thought I'm going to learn something here, but it was a club full of nutters! The coach was an absolute lunatic called Tom Whalley, and he was more eccentric and off-the-wall than anything I'd seen at Halifax. There wasn't any big change, it was a real family club, Watford, I loved it but it was only Halifax Town in disguise, in the First Division because they'd climbed up from obscurity. They were in the Fourth Division just a few seasons before that and they'd built a couple of stands, there was one big difference, in that the crowds were much bigger, so you couldn't hear them... in the small crowds, you could hear them shouting out – 'Holden, you're rubbish!' – but in these massive crowds you can't hear anything, it's just a wall of noise, background noise – so that was one big difference.

***We had some great atmospheres at Boundary Park, you also played in front of the Kippax at Maine Road; are you conscious as a player of the atmosphere in the ground, and how that might have changed since the Premier League and all-seating?***

We definitely recognised it because those evening games, particularly in the cup at Boundary Park, the Chadderton Road end – I think there was a capacity of about 6,000 standing – they made enough noise for 30,000 fans. I can always remember, when we were attacking the Rochdale Road end, and turning back towards the Chadderton stand, there were all these lights going on, people smoking, the atmosphere was really electric. The Kippax was similar, but they didn't make as much noise as the Oldham mob did! Then when it changed, it went as flat as a pancake, the noise. In the old days, I can remember some of my Leeds mates saying that they used to meet by the fourth pillar in the Gelderd Road end at Leeds every week, and they'd all congregate there. But when it got to season tickets, they got spread out all round the ground, so they couldn't even sit next to each other, they had to go round asking people to swap – absolute farce. So it did change it dramatically, and it was Hillsborough that did it, Heysel as well, but it's definitely changed the atmosphere and it was a lot quieter when it went all-seater than when it was standing, that's for sure.

*You were at the peak of your career [moving from Oldham to Manchester City] just as the First Division became the Premier League – what did you as a player, and team-mates, think about it at the time, did you talk about it?*

We did discuss it and we thought it was a load of bullshit, changing the name from the First Division to the Premiership was just trying to glamorise it – let's make it sound French, like food sounds better in French! They came up with this idea that it'd benefit the national side, who were having a torrid time – they'd had a decent '90 World Cup, but prior to that they didn't really do much, from 1970 to '86 they weren't too hot at all. [Qualifying for] '94 was a disaster, so there was this urban myth that it would benefit the national side, and there's no real evidence of that. We just carried on as normal, we didn't see any significant changes, early on anyway – I don't think the money got big until '96, '97 so we didn't get any benefits from the money. We just cracked on and thought nothing of it, really. It annoyed me that they started talking about 'founder members of the Premier League' – the founder members of the Football League will ever remain, but to me the Premier League was just a transition of name. Even Oldham get put in that, 'founder member' – bullshit! They were just in the old First Division and worked their way there on merit.

They built homogenous stadia – when you were a fan, you could recognise every ground by the floodlights, the stands, the cornices they had on, those beautiful things, real places with character, and now they're just the same. Wembley to me is not what it was, I'm not a fan of the new Wembley at all, why they couldn't preserve the towers – it's like knocking the bloody Parthenon down! It's a crying shame, because each ground was a special place, unique.

## *Who were the best players you played with or against, and your most difficult opponents?*

It's changed slightly as I've re-evaluated it over the years, but for me the best player, pound-for-pound, for skill, pace and what he could do, was definitely Ian Marshall, Andy Ritchie was excellent, and Neil Redfearn too. The best I played against, for sheer shock value, was Paul Gascoigne and another guy called Krasimir Balakov, Bulgarian international, he wore the number ten shirt, not Stoichkov, because he was better than Stoichkov! The most difficult defenders tended to be people like Warren Barton, he was hard work, whereas Paul Parker was less difficult, Barker at QPR and Denis [Irwin] was hard work, when he was playing for United, although I did get the better of him in that semi-final in '94 although Den will argue against that! In my ten-year career I played against lots of great players and with lots of great players, and the only thing I can't understand is why it never and still does not translate to a winning national team.

## *If you'd had the chance, would you have been interested in playing in a different country – was there a particular league, or country, that you would have preferred, given the choice?*

I might have said France – I'm not bad at French! I can manage to get through a conversation in French. I liked the idea, I got taken to a game when I was a youngster, we went to France a lot on holiday, my dad was a Francophile, and my mother was, and we did summer holidays there from when I was about 6 or 7 through to 12, 13. He took me to watch a game, Auxerre vs St Etienne, we'd stopped at a camp-site at Auxerre overnight, and I really liked the atmosphere – it didn't kick off until 10 at night, you know, it was brilliant. So I liked the idea of French football, they had some magnificent players in the late 90s/noughties, and they've come back again, haven't they? It's a great way of life, as well – I could have stuck that for a few years at the end of my career, but it never happened, I ended up at Blackpool!

## *What aspects of the game have improved?*

A lot of things have changed for the better, obviously the pitches – some of the pitches I played on, if you go on to YouTube and watch Halifax Town v Wolves, I think 1988, the pitch looks like the Luftwaffe have just done some practice on it! Horse of the Year Show job, like that 1970 FA Cup Final, Leeds v Chelsea, Wednesday night they had the Horse of the Year Show at Wembley, and on Saturday they played the Cup Final on it – imagine that now! Football kits are better, they're lighter. I'm not impressed with the colour of the boots but then if you're going to wear pink you've got to be Lionel Messi, you've got to be good enough. Even now, when I coach now, I've got a pair of old-style Pumas, modern but black, you know with the white Puma bit on them and the little cat, I also have a pair of Adidas – black with the three stripes. To me, they're football boots. I did go against my principles a bit when I signed for Watford, I got a three grand-a-year deal with Diadora to wear their boots, and unfortunately they had a yellow streak down them, took a bit of getting used to. The balls are better, the goalposts are better, the stadiums certainly aren't because they've lost their character, so there's swings and roundabouts to it. Money has gone out of hand, it is daft money although they are getting heavily taxed, there's no way you can get away with that. Has it made them less hungry to bust a gut if they're on 17 grand a week just playing in the under-21s or reserves? Does that make you want to drop down a couple of divisions to prove yourself? It's been glamorised out of all proportion nowadays.

In all the decades of the Football League there have always been top players who would have been the top players in any generation of the game. The pitches and equipment have changed, the training methods and coaching has changed and the money and coverage has changed! The management has changed and how they play the game has changed. The owners and even the names of the leagues have changed. But talent will always be there and so will the die-hard fans so football will survive no matter what they do to it, I have faith in that!

# Gerry Stewart

Gerry was born in 1946 in Dundee and spent seven years as a goalkeeper with Preston North End before playing for Barnsley and Boston United. He worked for many years at Leeds Metropolitan University (Carnegie) and is now retired.

## What are your earliest football memories?

I was, still am in a sense unfortunately, a mad Dundee fan – not Dundee United, absolutely not. Dundee United in the 50s were nothing, they were kept going by some genius who invented what they called the 'Tay Pools' locally, which made a hell of a lot of money and kept them going. Dundee were the team, although not when I first started watching them – my brother would take me – and the star player in those days was Billy Steel, he played a number of games for Scotland. But come the end of the 50s, and into the very early 60s, when I'm 14, 15, all of a sudden they had a great team – this is the team that won the Championship for the first and only time in their history [in 1962]. I can rattle off the team now: Linney, Hamilton, Cox, Seith, Ure, Wishart, Smith, Penman, Cousin, Gilzean, Robertson. Of all those guys, Gilzean would have been my hero, he was everyone's hero. That same team, in their first-ever venture into Europe, got to the semi-final. Their first game was against Cologne, a highly-rated German team, and they won 8-1 in the first game and lost 4-0 in the second and I think the Germans missed a penalty. By then, I had gone down to Preston for trials.

If anything, I couldn't have cared if I became a player or not, I was such a fan of Dundee – that could have been my life. It would have been a bloody sad one, just watching them get worse and worse, but these early memories are all effectively built around Dundee Football Club.

## *What was your route into the Football League, from Scotland to Preston – can you explain how that came about?*

I was only at Butterburn [a junior club] for 12 to 15 months, as luck would have it, because we had these two teams in the under-16s league and I was in the under-15s to start with. I went immediately into the under-16s even though I wasn't old enough, and then they had an evening game in the under-18s league, where again they had an under-17s team and under-18s. And of course twice in the season they'd have to play each other, and one night the under-17s keeper was injured or something, so they asked me to play against my own club, albeit the older lads. That night there happened to be a scout there, and I played well. In a sense I was extremely lucky, because in my under-16s team, we were so good, we'd beat every team in the league – 7/8/9/10, or 11-0 – and I'd have bugger all to do. I mean it was boring, I'd end up throwing mud pies at the centre-half, nothing to do. I could never, ever have been spotted by a scout playing in the team that I was supposed to play for because I never had anything to do, they were so good. Only that night, where I happened to play for the under-17s against the under-18s, did there happen to be a scout there, and the next thing they invited me down to Preston for trials. I was 15, I had my 16th birthday in Preston.

So I'm down there at 15, and Preston are still a big club, gradually going down but only relegated from the First Division a couple of seasons before [1960/61], and I was there in 1962. Tommy Finney had retired by then and the club was going down a bit. But they used to have hundreds of triallists. So I went down there, and in those days as was the norm when there was a lot of manufacturing industry, I worked in the shipyard [in Dundee] and of course the city would close down for two weeks. Quite the norm in most cities, England and Scotland as well, so that was it, the Dundee holiday fortnight and I'm going down for a trial for two weeks. To be honest, it didn't go that well – I was very good, despite my size, at taking crosses, but allegedly I wasn't so good on the ground. They pointed that out to me, that they were very pleased with what I was doing, but was there any possible reason why I might not be as good at diving? The only excuse I could come up with was, 'well it is the summer' and the grounds are baked by this time and in training, my trainer would say 'don't bother diving for it cause you'll only skin all your legs.' Can you imagine giving that as an excuse? But it was the only honest one I could come up with. At the end of the fortnight they said 'look, we're not that convinced, why don't you stay for another week' and it was no skin off my nose, I never gave a second thought to it.

So I stayed for another week and at the end of it, it was more or less 'don't call us, we'll call you – work hard and come back next year' – that's the brush-off I suspect they give to all kids, just to help break the sadness. So that was it, I was going home and I went out with some of my new-found friends the night before, to a café somewhere, and came back and there was a message that had been left for me, which is 'you've got to stay for another month.' I didn't know what had happened, but it was then I twigged, what about my job? Well, I'd lost my job because I'd been away for a fortnight, I hadn't told them, no-one had told my employer in the shipyard and I just didn't turn up so they bloody sacked me! My father worked in the shipyard, he couldn't do anything about it so I think he got on the phone fairly angry at Preston North End, 'you've taken him down there, made him stay an extra week, he's lost his job, what are you going to do about it?' I think they were feeling so guilty about it they said 'OK, stay for another month, work hard' – the rest you might say is history, in as much at the end of that month, yes they agreed to accept me.

## *Did you go straight on to a professional contract, or was it as an apprentice?*

That's another interesting little tit-bit. In those days the Scottish Football Association had a rule, principally at the behest of Rangers and Celtic, as you can imagine. They had been moaning about the number of Scots schoolboys that were going to England, so Rangers and Celtic couldn't get their hands on those kids. Another one who played with me in the Dundee schools team was Peter Lorimer, he's off to Leeds, but hundreds, maybe even thousands over a decade, of Scottish schoolboys were going to English clubs, there were scouts all over the place. They were getting fed up with this, they got the Scottish Football Association to impose, not a ban but a condition on the

English clubs. The English lads were all what you would call apprentice professionals until they were 18. I signed a professional form at 17 – this was the condition that the Scottish FA had put on the English clubs, you cannot take these kids down and keep them as apprentices, you have to offer them a contract at 17 or get rid of them. During that period between 15 and 17 – as I say, I started at 15 – they had me down as an apprentice painter, that was the way they would overcome it. Although you were getting paid as a professional, they had you down as a member of the ground staff – I never picked a bloody paint-brush up – and I suspect most of the English clubs were doing the same. So yes, a professional at 17 but essentially at 15, just not so that everyone would know.

### *When did you make your debut for Preston, and what do you remember of the game?*

[19/11/1966] It was a game full of drama as well, it was against Wolves who were promoted from the Second Division that season. Preston had five teams and I'd been in the fifth team at the beginning, and I'd progressed through fairly quickly into the reserve team, and the reserve goalkeeper [John Barton] had been sold to Blackburn Rovers. So I was in the reserves, and there I languished for many a year! Alan Kelly was the first-team goalkeeper, the head of what you might call the Kelly dynasty – his sons Gary and Alan both became professional goalkeepers, Alan played for Sheffield United and Ireland, his dad played for Ireland many times. I made my debut, not because he was injured but I think he was playing for the Republic of Ireland – they didn't do what they do now and play midweek, so he played for his country and I made my debut against Wolves. They were probably top of the league at the time. The first thing you notice is just the noise, it's incredible, even when you're having your kick-about before the match, the noise is unbelievable. You could be screaming at someone five yards away and they wouldn't hear you, and the singing, I've never experienced that, it was a buzz alright.

They beat us 3-2 with the last kick of the game, which was a penalty – it's a refurbished ground, but if you see old photos of Molineux, there's a clock on the stand and on that clock it was 5 to 5. Now, never did a game go on until then – nowadays with all the added time you might manage it, but never in those days. They beat us 3-2, they were 2-0 up and we pulled it back to 2-each but they got a dubious penalty, the last kick of the game. I'd had a good game. The other debutant that day was a guy called Phil Parkes, Wolves keeper – both of us were making our debuts in the same game. I rushed from the dressing room, I knew I'd had a fairly good game, to listen to the radio, the old Sports Report and yes, I got a good mention. That was really quite something, my debut.

***How was it with Alan Kelly always being first choice, that must have been a little bit frustrating?***

Well, ultimately, I had seven years as understudy. He was a great goalkeeper. Yeah, unbelievably frustrating. Although I only played about four league games, I'd play a lot of friendlies and tour matches and things like that, but he'd never get injured and there were no subs, no rotation, nothing like that. Of those games, I think three were because he was representing the Republic of Ireland, and one was he was at his mother's funeral. He was a big mate of mine, really very, very friendly, we trained together and I admired him enormously. Wonderful man, fantastic keeper, consistent – he hardly made a mistake – he'd have got into most international teams, never mind the Republic of Ireland, who at that time weren't a great footballing nation.

In the end the frustration boiled over because we went through a few managers – the original one was Jimmy Milne – Preston North End was always a big club for Scots, the manager was from Dundee, the scout who picked me up was from Dundee. We didn't get relegated under Jimmy Milne – his son was Gordon Milne, who was a good player for Liverpool – but we were going nowhere. So they brought in Bobby Seith, who'd been in that Dundee team I mentioned, he'd been a coach at Rangers, he came to Preston as manager for a couple of years but then we got relegated. Then we got Alan Ball [Senior] and that's Preston in the Third Division, probably for the first time in their history but only for a year, we won the Championship that year. But again, I still wasn't breaking through and though Kelly was in his thirties and wasn't going to be a long-term perspective, he was still fit enough to be as good as he was. The frustration boiled over, and the manager and I just did not see eye to eye, not at all – I had many a spat with him.

One of my frustrations was I couldn't get in the team, but he wouldn't consent to transfer me. I'd asked for a transfer, you more or less had to do that in those days – you had to somehow get them to put you on a transfer list in order for clubs to give you any attention. Part of the problem was that they could tell you that you were on the transfer list, but you'd no evidence – I suspected he hadn't put me on the list, and it just all boiled over. Now you're talking about dramatic changes in the contractual terms and conditions of players, in those days a club could still retain your registration as long as they offered you a contract which was in no way inferior to the one that had expired. They didn't have to offer you more, they just couldn't offer you less or you had a right to leave. If they offered you the same, you had no right to leave – you could go and work on a building site, but they retained your registration, hence the name, the 'retain and transfer' system. It was all one way. As far as I know, no-one ever signed more than a two-year contract, so you'd have two years and a two-year option, but the option was the club's, not the player's.

Mine had come to the end and I was offered terms, and I refused because by this time I knew what I was going to do. I was going to go to a tribunal because I knew he [Alan Ball Sr] was bullshitting me, telling me I was on the transfer list. I was playing well, really well, and nothing was happening. I think what they're frightened of very often is letting players go, who eventually do well and make them look a bit stupid.

So I went to an industrial tribunal at the FA headquarters, down in London and I was asking for a free transfer. That's what I really wanted because I'd already arranged with one of my former coaches who'd become a manager, albeit at Crewe Alexandra. This guy was a famous name, Dennis Viollet, one of the Busby Babes. I liked Dennis, he liked me, I played well for him – you get that, there are people who treat you in a particular way and it makes you play well, and there are others who rub you up the wrong way, and have the opposite effect. Dennis was manager at Crewe and we'd informally talked about, if I could get away from Preston, but it would have to be a free transfer because they couldn't afford it. It would be a free, but I would get money because they wouldn't have to pay a fee for me.

I went to the tribunal, submitted all my documentation – it wouldn't have been the most articulate stuff you've ever read, I left school at 15, how could I articulate a case? I was represented by the Professional Footballers' Association Chairman, Cliff Lloyd, but he was only part of a panel of three or four, one of them was a Lord. You're just a working-class kid stuck in front of these people asking questions that you really don't know, and Cliff Lloyd's doing his best but ultimately they didn't grant me a free transfer but they did say to Preston North End 'now he goes on the list, officially.' Apparently they'd said 'we could sell him to a dozen clubs tomorrow' but I didn't know this until afterwards – they said 'he's on the list and you circulate the list to every club in the country, now he's for transfer.' I signed the following day for Barnsley. I wish I hadn't have done.

The only good thing I can say about Barnsley Football Club is that they made me give the game up at a full-time professional level, that's how bad they were. I went to night school, I went to University and the rest is history – I'm an extremely happy individual – so the move to Barnsley in that sense was a wonderful one, but not because of Barnsley Football Club. They were so bloody bad that I decided I was giving it up. I was so desperate to get away from Preston, I never even looked to see where they were, they were the first club that came in and I negotiated something. I probably would have made a few bob, I twisted Preston's arm and they gave me something to send me on my way but I never even looked. This was October [1971] so the season was a couple of months old, they were bottom of the league, played 9 games and had 4 points, lost about 25 goals – not too surprising that they wanted a new keeper! It was awful, but I actually played well and had a really good first season. We went down on goal average, as it was in those days, not goal difference, and if I'm not mistaken we had more points than we scored goals. Since it was only two points for a win, you might want to ask yourself the question, 'where did all the bloody points come from?' A lot of them came from no-score draws. At one point I think we went twelve games without scoring.

## *Who was the manager at the time?*

A guy called John McSeveney, another Scot. He was alright McSeveney, and I played for him, I played well. We actually had a good defence, I rated the guys. Barry Murphy, a guy called David Booth who went to Grimsby eventually, a good left-back, Eric Winstanley at centre-half, he went to Chesterfield, we had a good defence. It's difficult to say you enjoyed relegation, because you don't, but I played well that year. Then the injuries started – over the course of the next three years I had two broken arms, two cartilage operations, some broken fingers, and even then over the four years I bet I only missed 20-30 games, but it was a dreadful club.

Coming from Preston North End, which was a big club in those days, you went into the dressing-room and all your kit was there, ironed, hung up ready for you, boots cleaned – and we all went through that as kids on the ground staff, we used to clean everyone else's boots, but when you hit the big time, you get the kids to clean your boots. So I had been used to all of that. When I went to Barnsley, I had a good debut down at Brighton, no-score draw, and turned up for training on Monday expecting the same. 'Where's your kit?' – 'what do you mean?' – 'haven't you brought any kit with you?' – 'don't tell me you don't provide me with kit' – 'where do think you are?' It went like that, and they went and got me some half-arsed gear from somewhere, bloody old pair of boots, absolutely dreadful.

## *How did Boston fit into that, how did that move come about?*

Boston were already a good club, I think if you check on the Northern Premier League they won the Championship four years out of six. They'd won it a couple of years when Jim Smith and Howard Wilkinson played, and was perhaps even assistant manager to Jim Smith. Jim had moved on to the big time by then, and Wilko took over as player-manager and he's living in and around South Yorkshire, in Sheffield, so I suppose he knew me over the years, seen and heard certain things. I think I was his first signing, I remember meeting him off the motorway somewhere south of Sheffield. For me it was something to help through University, though I was getting a grant – in the good old days when you got a grant – and it was a good team, I think we won the Championship the following two years and a whole host of other trophies.

Arguably unofficially, the best non-league team in the country. Justification for that is, at the end of the year you'd have the Northern Premier League Champions play the Southern Premier League Champions – and the first year we won the Championship, we were playing against Wimbledon FC over two legs, and we beat them. So we were officially the best non-league team in the country. I think the second time we did it, we played against Bath and they beat us over two legs. As for Wimbledon, within a decade of playing us they'd won the FA Cup – what an extraordinary rise, absolutely unbelievable!

## *How would you compare the standard of the Northern Premier League to the Football League – did you notice a difference?*

No, by the time I left Barnsley they were in the Fourth Division and the standard there wasn't that high, the best of the non-league teams would match them. For clubs that wanted to get into the League, in those days there was no automatic promotion and relegation, that didn't exist. For non-league there was the Northern Premier League, which is what it was deemed to be, the best of the northern clubs, and the southern equivalent. But even having won that play-off [between the non-league champions], that didn't get you into the Football League. What got you into the League was the 92 League clubs voting and either there must have been enormous pressures put on them to vote for a particular club, or they would choose one which suited them. Now Boston, Lincolnshire – why would the Football League clubs want to go there, even once a season, out in the sticks? I used to argue that we were clearly doing it on the pitch, but the marketing was horrendous, they weren't going round bigging us up and getting clubs interested. In reality, they were never going to vote for Boston United.

Wigan [runners-up to Boston in 1977-78], on the other hand – we beat them four times that year, we knocked them out of the cups and beat them home and away in the league, and they got voted into the Football League. How did they manage that? Well, Wigan, it's in the middle of everybody and again, it's an incredible success story for them with Dave Whelan [the owner], winning the FA Cup twenty years later, an extraordinary rise. We beat them four times out of four and we stayed in the Northern Premier League while they went into the Football League. I'm not absolutely convinced that Boston wanted to get into the Football League, they certainly didn't seem to me to want to make that much of an effort. Eventually of course they did get there, through the Conference [in 2002], the automatic route.

I had five years at Boston and I absolutely loved it. I don't know if it was because the pressure was off, whether it was being a bigger fish in a small pond. I loved the camaraderie with the lads. There was a lot of travelling involved for me, I was going from Leeds twice a week, we'd train down at Newark, so that was a long round trip, home games were a couple of hundred miles round trip, but Boston treated us ever so well. In comparison to Barnsley, they would put us in nice hotels, the best food everywhere you went. The old man Malkinson [Chairman], he wasn't too shy if we were getting beat at half-time, 'come on lads, if you win this game, there'll be a few more bob.' I mean, that's not an incentive to be honest, you either want to win or you don't. Often an extra £4 or £6 isn't going to turn you from being a crap player to a great player, but he did it, his heart was in the right place and he treated us well.

### *What were the training facilities like at your clubs, and was there any specialist goalkeeping coaching?*

Not really a goalkeeping coach as such, I would learn from Alan Kelly and as a young lad, we were allocated someone on the ground staff, that was an ex-player called George Bargh. To some extent, there wasn't specialist anything! The people who were employed by the football clubs, as was my experience certainly at Preston in the earliest of years – as I was leaving, it had started to change. Back then, those people employed on the football side were ex-players who'd clearly had a good career with the club. But in terms of what they knew, all they knew was what had been taught to them, going back 20 years – so you're in say 1963/64, but you've got a guy who's just retired and whose career was between 1944 and 1964. And I bet when he started in 1944, he had a coach who was playing in 1924. So not only was there no coaching of football as you understood it, all you had – and they might have spent one day a week getting you fit – we had a place at Deepdale called 'Little Wembley' behind a big fence, and there wasn't a blade of grass on it, covered in bloody mud. So we'd go and have first team against reserves there, the young lads would play there, a place for some ball skills, but before we'd go on there, they'd tell us to run round the track at Deepdale as a warm-up. We'd go round once, and then expect to go in the tunnel, so if we were asked to go round again we'd say 'what, are you trying to kill us?'

It was so rudimentary, you would not believe it, the facilities up at Preston – the 'gym,' it had some wall bars and I hung on those wall bars many a day because they were trying to stretch me, to get me taller – I've still got the marks. They had a couple of dumbbells in there, a medicine ball that was burst, and you might go in there and do some exercises, maybe run around and do something stupid for a bit, but coaching? No, there was none. Even the treatment of injuries, they hadn't got a clue. Obviously the most common injury would be something like you'd twisted your ankle. Behind what they called the 'treatment room,' where they did have a machine, ultrasound or whatever, they had a room where it was like a little Belfast sink, and what they did was, put a bucket of ice water at the side of it, and make that absolutely boiling hot. So you'd stick your ankle in the boiling hot, take it out and stick it in the bucket of ice, and you'd spend all your time doing that – that's about the only treatment they knew.

As the decade went on, there was something happening, and I have a feeling it was coming from the likes of West Ham United, who had always been known to be a good footballing side. I think one of the main individuals was Malcolm Allison, and he of course moved from West Ham to Manchester City, with Joe Mercer, and they had a good team. I think the embryonic professionalism was starting to get in vogue, they would start to talk to you about your diet, and we got a guy named Peter Keeling, who had been an Olympic athlete – never won anything, but he'd represented Great Britain in the Commonwealth Games and maybe an Olympics. They employed him to come and make us run with a purpose, that was under Alan Ball [Sr] and he was a big fan of Malcolm Allison, so something was happening.

I then remember they employed a physiotherapist, a guy who seemed to know what he was doing – before that we had Willie Cunningham, an old Scottish footballer, a miner, bloody arms like this, legs like tree trunks. He was the reserve team coach/trainer, and if you went to him with your injury, he'd be 'where is it?' They had to scrape you off the ceiling – and the delight on his face when he found where it hurt you! He didn't have a clue whether he was doing you any good or not. As I say, there was no real professionalism until towards the end of the 60s, it was emerging. Peter Keeling would make you do all these sorts of runs, and they had something called the Harvard test, where they'd make you go up and down and then take your pulse, tell you to rest, then take your pulse again – this was allegedly to find out whether, as it were, you were kidding them on, because if your pulse rate had got so far back down to its low level, it's clear that your recovery rate was superb and you weren't working hard enough! So they had us doing some very strenuous running – I hated it – and then do all this pseudo-scientific testing stuff, whether or not you were getting fitter. But that didn't come in until, I would say, '69, '70, '71 – maybe at other clubs it had started earlier, but it was only just getting round to Preston North End.

### *Was the goalkeeper targeted when you were playing, at set-pieces and things?*

Yes, certainly early on they'd try to put you under a degree of pressure, to see whether you'd buckle. They'd be prepared [to foul], if they could get away with it fine, but if not they'd still make you worry about what was going to happen at corners and the like. Either you had the bottle to deal with it or you didn't.

### *What was Howard Wilkinson like to work with, and would you have said at the time he had the potential to go on to have the career he had?*

Yes, I could, and what became surprising was the kind of thing that he ultimately got criticised for was this 'route one' stuff. His time at Boston was spent being a good coach, and insistent on passing, playing it out from the back – to the point where I'd get a really good bollocking if I was kicking it out from hand. The idea where he'd get criticised for 'route one' stuff was strange to me, because it's not how he was. He was well respected, he was a player-coach and he did his bit, he was a hard worker – he was a winger – he was just one of the players when he was on the pitch. There seemed to be something going on with an individual called Wing Commander [Charles] Reep, and he had done some statistical analysis that suggested that most goals came from mistakes in the penalty area, and therefore his idea was to get everything into the penalty area and it'll break down – you get it and you'll score. 70% of all goals came from two passes or less, it was this kind of thing. So at some point, clearly Howard got sucked into this and I think that's the origin of this long ball stuff.

*One of the main the changes from your playing days, and even since the Premier League, is physical contact – it seems to have gone from one extreme, where there was not enough protection for the more skilful players especially, to the other, where free-kicks are given for virtually any physical contact. What's your take on that?*

To watch football today, I think it's magnificent, the skill levels are, for me, exceptional. I've had this discussion with old team-mates, and a guy called Tony Morley [Aston Villa and England], I was waxing lyrical and he said 'but look at the pitches we played on, how were we ever going to exhibit those sort of skills?' And yeah, I remember places like the Baseball Ground, the only place where you found any grass was on the four corners. Deepdale was a good pitch, a beautiful pitch – Oakwell was even better at Barnsley, and Leeds Road, Huddersfield, that was great. But some of those other pitches, they were just quagmires. So there may be something in that, but I just think the level of skill today is phenomenal. There would be a lot of emphasis in my earliest days in players kicking each other, say to Willie [Cunningham] 'you've got a flying winger against you today' – 'well he can't run without legs' and occasionally there would be tackles like that.

At Burnley – that was a good club, boy did they punch above their weight, they were a good team in the early 60s – they had a couple of wingers, [Johnny] Price and Willie Morgan, and they were so good. You had the football pitch, the grounds with a minimum and a maximum, well you could alter the size of it if you wanted, so they'd bring the pitch in and the wingers were less effective, but even less effective if you kicked them! There were a lot of full-backs, certainly, doing that.

Leeds United, the team that got promoted to the First Division with Revie – and that year [1963/64], Leeds and Sunderland got promoted and Preston North End finished third, and got to the Cup Final – that was a dirty team, and the first team he had in the First Division was too. They were always physical thereafter, and they were hated, absolutely hated – most of the hate I think was about jealousy, cause they were good, they were a great team, absolutely magnificent. They should have won a lot more than they did, but they were a very physical team. Chelsea were a physical team, the Harrises.

I understand people saying 'oh, the old days,' but the old days weren't as good as what we're seeing now. However good Tom Finney was, what's Messi like, what's Ronaldo like? What these guys give you in a game of football, it's phenomenal. I rarely watch the Premier League, but when I do see it, the skill is fantastic. And they're all so athletic – you'll not go back before 1970 and see players doing a somersault after they've scored a goal! Some of these guys are amazing, they look real athletes. Their ability to control the ball, it's instant – but then, the ball's different.

As a goalkeeper, it'd be difficult, partly because of the ball but what would drive me nuts is the new offside rules. This business of players being in front of you all the time, and being deemed not to be interfering. That used to be one of the biggest fears you'd have as a goalkeeper, not being able to see, can't see the ball – for me, if I could see the ball, and see someone lifting back, ready to strike the ball, I've got a chance.

### *How conscious were you as a player of the noise from the terraces and the atmosphere in the ground?*

Very conscious of it, I loved playing with big crowds, it was a real adrenalin rush. I wouldn't be any the less nervous – I tended to be fairly nervous before games – but once I got out there, there's no better thing. And if you're playing well, and they're on your back, screaming at you... I actually loved playing in front of sizable crowds – unfortunately I didn't play in front of that many but if you think, Barnsley against Villa in the Third Division, there'd be about 36,000 at Villa Park. They won the Championship that year, went back up to the Second Division.

## *Who were the best players you played with or against?*

Maybe a couple of weeks before George Best made his debut for Man United [September 1963], and I explained that Preston had five teams, all these big clubs had five teams, and they were in the Lancashire Leagues. The first team in the Football League, the Central League for the reserves, and then the Lancashire Leagues, Divisions One, Two and Three. George Best never played for Manchester United reserves, skipped them, and I think a fortnight before he made his debut, he played against us and it was a story of him scoring a particularly spectacular goal. But we didn't know who he was, he just played for Manchester United, and then after two or three weeks somebody said 'that's the kid who scored that goal against us, remember that goal?' So yeah, I played against Bestie!

Who else? I was in digs when I first went to Preston, so this was in 1962, and we had a guy who became a great player, was a great player then, called Peter Thompson [England 1966 World Cup squad]. I was in digs with Pete, and he turned out to be a great player in that famous Liverpool team, Shanks' team. Also on the ground staff with me, a guy called Howard Kendall, played in the '64 Cup Final against West Ham, one of the youngest players ever. He was an amazing, precocious talent, wasn't particularly quick but just seemed to be everywhere the ball was going to go, could read a game, great passing ability. Very, very good player.

Archie Gemmill was at Preston, most of the time in the reserves, but he got an under-23 cap [for Scotland] and that was the making of him, I think it was up at Sunderland and Cloughie was watching, and came and got him. Despite the great goal he scored for Scotland against Holland, to some extent he wasn't a great dribbler, but I'd seen him do that kind of thing before. My theory is not that he had control, but because he'd just about lost control, what he was, was unbelievably quick over these short distances. To all intents and purposes, he'd lost control, so that the opponent would think 'this is mine,' not realising this little sod would get there before them. I mean, you'd want him in your team, his work-rate was tremendous.

Peter Lorimer as a schoolboy, a different school from me, but we made our debuts in the city schools team. Yeah, he was another precocious talent, the goals he would score in a year – he wasn't particularly big, but he was powerful and just an ability to strike a ball. He used to take these free-kicks 30, 35 yards out – God knows what he'd be like with a modern ball.

## Bibliography and Sources

Les Back, Tim Crabbe, and John Solomos, *The Changing Face of Football: Racism, Identity,* and *Multiculture in the English game* (Berg, 2001)

Matthew Bazell, *Theatre of Silence: The Lost Soul of Football* (Pegasus Elliot Mackenzie, 2008)

Bryon Butler, *The Official Illustrated History of the Football League* (Blitz Editions, 1993)

R. C. Churchill, *Sixty Seasons of League Football* (Penguin, 1958)

Richard Crooks, *Grandad, What Was Football Like in the 1970s?* (Pitch, 2017)

Hunter Davies, *Postcards from the Edge of Football: A Social History of a British Game* (Mainstream, 2010)

Ken Ferris, *Football Terms and Teams* (Carcanet Press, 2005)

David Goldblatt, *The Game of Our Lives: The Meaning and Making of English Football* (Penguin, 2015)

Arthur Hopcraft, *The Football Man: People and Passions in Soccer* (Aurum Press, 2013; original edition Collins, 1968)

Simon Inglis, *Football Grounds of England & Wales* (1st Ed.; HarperCollinsWillow, 1983)

Simon Inglis, *Football Grounds of Britain* (3rd Ed.; CollinsWillow, 1996)

Anthony King, *The Premier League and the New Consumption of Football* (Ph.D. Thesis, University of Salford Institute for Social Research, 1995)

Anthony King, *The End of the Terraces: The Transformation of English Football in the 1990s* (Leicester University Press, 1998)

Scott Murray, *The Title: The Story of the First Division* (Bloomsbury, 2017)

Emy Onuora, *Pitch Black: The Story of Black British Footballers* (Biteback, 2015)

Ian Plenderleith, *Rock 'n' Roll Soccer: The Short Life and Fast Times of the North American Soccer League* (Icon Books, 2014)

David Russell, *Football and the English: A Social History of Association Football in England, 1863-1995* (Carnegie Publishing, 1997)

Dave Twydell, *Rejected F.C. Volume 1: Histories of the Ex-Football League Clubs* (Yore Publications, 1988)

Simon Tyers, *Restricted View – Football On British TV Before The Premier League* (download at https://bigmatchaction.blogspot.com/, 2020)

James Walvin, *The People's Game: A Social History of British Football* (Allen Lane, 1975)

James Walvin, *Football and the Decline of Britain* (Macmillan, 1986)

Andrew Ward and John Williams, *Football Nation: Sixty Years of the Beautiful Game* (Bloomsbury, 2009)

Jonathan Wilson, *Inverting the Pyramid: The History of Soccer Tactics* (Orion, 2014)

*British Football and Social Change* (edited by John Williams and Stephen Wagg; Leicester University Press, 1991)

*Football Cultures and Identities* (edited by Gary Armstrong and Richard Giulianotti; Macmillan, 1999)

*The Park Drive Book of Football 1968* (edited by Gordon Banks)

*The Sportsman's World of Soccer* (Marshall Cavendish, 1975)

*The Story of The Football League: An Official History Published in Commemoration of the Fiftieth Anniversary of its Formation* – Compiled by Charles E. Sutcliffe, J. A. Brierley and F. Howarth (The Football League, Preston, 1938)

Various editions of *The Football League Review,* c. 1970 to 1974

Various football annuals, magazines (primarily *Match, Shoot!* and *Soccer Monthly*) and match programmes, c. 1955-93

Various editions of *Rothmans Football Yearbook,* 1971/72 to 1992/93